As I sat in the retreat house in the Northern Mountains at Hungary reading Luke Davis' recent work, I realized that Luke's ability as a fiction writer and his love of the history of the church have been perfectly wed. Davis has produced a volume that provides a helpful survey of missions since the reformation. Creating narratives that make the lives of gospel proclaimers come to life, the author makes the lives of the well known as well as the not so well known accessible to the reader.

As a missiologist and a practitioner, I give God glory for the way *Renewal* gives the reader a global view of missions. But, service without sound theological insight can create chaos. Knowing this, Davis has masterfully woven just enough theological insight into this work. Thus the reader will discover that mission is born out of theology that understands the plan and call of God. It is my hope that readers will listen as they read for God to call them. For I can tell you, that the fields remain white unto harvest, and the workers are both few and dwindling. I hope that God will use this volume to show any reader, not just the young, that God may use them for the cause of the kingdom in places where the gospel is wanting.

Rev. Dr. Thomas Foley
Executive Director, Christian Educators Outreach

In this volume of Luke Davis's Risen Hope series, the reader has a chance to see history unfold through the 16th, 17th, and 18th centuries. The church has been reinvigorated by the Reformation and is now reaching out with the good news of the Gospel. Politicians, churchmen, and missionaries are just a few of the people the reader will meet in these pages. Each story is vividly told so that the reader learns how the Gospel impacted each person and the world around them.

Linda Finlayson
Author of *G*[illegible]*line*

In this volume, Luke Davis uses his biographical skills to take us on a journey through the 17th to the 19th centuries. Once again, as in his previous volumes, he brings his characters colourfully to life, and stimulates us to want to know more about their persons and their times, in those three epoch-making centuries of church history.

Dr Nick Needham
Church History tutor,
Highland Theological College, Dingwall, Scotland

RENEWAL

THE CHURCH EXPANDS OUTWARD

LUKE H. DAVIS

CF4·K

10 9 8 7 6 5 4 3 2 1

Paperback ISBN: 978-1-5271-0993-3
Ebook ISBN: 978-1-5271-1038-0

Published by Christian Focus Publications,
Geanies House, Fearn, Tain, Ross-shire,
IV20 1TW, Scotland, U.K.
www.christianfocus.com;
email: info@christianfocus.com

Design and illustrations: Laura K Sayers
Cover designer: Catriona Mackenzie

Printed and bound by
Bell and Bain, Glasgow

Scripture quotations are taken from the King James Version of the Bible.

CONTENTS

Dedicated with love for and in memory of
four of God's most wonderful gifts,
my grandparents

Daryl and Mary Davis

and

Wayne and Frances Herron

for proclaiming the Gospel in words,
for showing the Gospel in example,
for every provision you made for me.

IMPORTANT MOMENTS IN THE AGE OF EXPANSION

1603

Queen Elizabeth I dies; James I becomes King of England

1607

English settlers found Jamestown in America

1611

The King James Version of the Bible is published

1620

English Pilgrims arrive in Plymouth Harbor in America

1632

Gustavus Adolphus of Sweden is killed in the Battle of Lutzen

1638

Cyril Lucaris is strangled to death in the Bosporus

1642

English Civil War (1642-1651)

1646

The Westminster Confession of Faith is drafted

1653

Oliver Cromwell begins to govern as Lord Protector of England
Beheading of King Charles I

1661

John Bunyan is jailed in Bedford County, England

1666

John Owen founds a congregation in London after the Great Fire

1683

The Winged Hussars help defeat the Ottomans at the Battle of Vienna

1721

Hans Egede arrives in Greenland as a Lutheran missionary

1743

David Brainerd begins missionary work amongst the Delaware Indians

1770

George Whitefield dies after preaching in Newburyport, Massachusetts

1781

Harry Hosier is the first Black man to preach a sermon in America

1807

The British Empire outlaws the slave trade via an Act of Parliament

1832

Emilie Mallet begins her charity work for young children and prisoners

1835

David Griffiths completes the translation of the Bible into the language of Madagascar

1837

Victoria becomes Queen of the United Kingdom

1841

Rabbi Duncan arrives in Hungary as a missionary to Jews there

1843

Soren Kierkegaard publishes *Either/Or* and *Fear and Trembling*

1851

Sojourner Truth addresses the Ohio Women's Rights Convention

1854

Charles Spurgeon becomes pastor of the New Park Street Chapel

1855

Dwight Moody becomes a Christian during a Sunday School class

1861

The American War Between the States begins

1865

Hudson Taylor founds the China Inland Mission

1899

The Boxer Rebellion begins, disrupting the China Inland Mission

THE AGE OF MISSION

Recently, I returned to the school where I serve to begin my twenty-fourth year in teaching. On the first day of every school year, there is an inevitable amount of energy mixed with confusion intertwined with anxiety. I see it on the faces of students who plunge through the hallways on the way to class. Whether spoken or silent, they have questions.

"Why did I get a locker on the bottom rather than on top?"

"What do I have during third hour?"

"Do I have Mr. Knerr or Mr. Skogen for history?"

"On what hallway is Precalculus?"

And the all-important inquiry...

"When is lunch?"

School is a shared experience, and the students are at one location, but they wonder where they should go and (many times) what is going on around them. We can often be part of something and yet still be amazed at how crazy and mixed-up it can be. We see people facing hardship, we encounter others with magnificent talents combined with great flaws, we view conflict and injustice around us, and we see others operating with passion to restore others' lives. So much energy, so much variety.

The Christian Church from the beginning of the seventeenth to the latter part of the nineteenth century was such an experience of dizzying vitality. It had been some time since followers of Jesus had seen such geographic expansion of the Gospel. One would have to go back to the ancient church to find such an advance of Christ's church over so much territory. However, the Protestant Reformation[1] created a new world

1. See book three in this series, *Reform: The Church at the Birth of Protestantism.*

among the nations of Europe religiously, socially, and culturally. The Catholic Church was no longer the undisputed leader in western Europe. The Roman Catholic leaders faced two possibilities: Fight hard against the Protestant believers or seek new places to extend their influence. Although there was verbal and military conflict between Catholics and Protestants, we also find Roman Catholic priests, monks, and teachers traveling to distant lands, preaching to, and converting people groups who had never encountered Christianity. Francis Xavier sailed to Japan, India, and Malaysia, establishing churches there under the Jesuit banner.[2] Bartolome de las Casas befriended, taught, and defended native tribes in the Caribbean. Jacques Marquette was a French priest who founded European settlements in Michigan, explored the Mississippi River valley, and preached fearlessly and compassionately to the Ojibwa, Huron, and Illinek tribes. In response to this missionary activity, Protestants (and Eastern Orthodox) believers were somewhat slow to react. Establishing their security within their regions was essential at first, but there is no doubt that when they sought to share the Gospel with others, they did so with a great deal of passion.

The first part of our story of the outward expansion of the Church displays a great deal of *hardship*. Cyril Lucaris found resistance to his teaching and leadership within the Orthodox Church, a resistance that had devastating consequences. John Owen suffered the loss of many of his children in infancy, and he sought to create a new church in London out of the devastation of the Great Fire. John Bunyan experienced a radical conversion but was then imprisoned by the established Church of England for illegal preaching. However, he found time in jail to write moving works of faith.

Other persons promoted conversion and sought to impress upon their hearers the hopelessness of their sinfulness and the great mercy found in Jesus to save them. Jonathan Edwards

---

2. The Jesuits were founded by Ignatius Loyola (1491-1556) and were dedicated educators and missionaries for the Catholic faith. The official name for the Jesuits is the *Society of Jesus*.

and George Whitefield tirelessly worked to preach Scripture to their listeners, helping them see the reality of human rebellion but always bringing them to a Savior who could rescue them from hell. David Brainerd encountered the Native Americans in the eastern United States and preached faithfully to them. Each man was marked by flaws which created difficulties in their ministries, but they never stopped believing that God could use them mightily in spite of their fallen nature.

Still others looked at the communities around them and the problems that struck at the heart of those places. Some desired to give freedom and hope to people seeking a new start. Others, such as Harry Hosier and Sojourner Truth, wanted to work on behalf of their people who were victims of injustice and wrongdoing. Leaders like William Wilberforce fought for years to end particular evils in society so others could be liberated. When French children were at risk in the waves of illness and plague, Emilie Mallet desired to give them a place to live, to learn, and be loved in the name of Christ.

And the Church kept pressing outward with a renewed zeal to reach the unconverted wherever they could be found. Charles Spurgeon transformed Victorian England with his powerful preaching. Missionaries took the light of God's grace to other lands, shown forth powerfully in the efforts of Robert Moffat in Africa and Hudson Taylor in China. Dwight Moody expended much energy throughout his life in bringing as many as he could into churches so they could experience the teaching and practical love of God.

Toward the end of the nineteenth century, we have a markedly different Church than at the close of the Reformation. It is a Church that expands outward. It is a Church of people seeking to be faithful to Christ in the circumstances they faced. It is a Church of people who are truly flawed and fallen. But what other people would God use for His purposes? And what an amazing story for Him to write, and what a journey that He calls us to join even now!

CYRIL LUCARIS

June 1638, Constantinople, Ottoman Empire

His white hair and long beard flew wildly around his head as the wind buffeted him with great force. The closer the Patriarch drew to the Topkapi Palace, the more ferociously the gale swept off the Sea of Marmara. Clenching his walking stick firmly in his right hand, Cyril Lucaris sighed as he wended his way toward the palace and his audience with the Sultan. The day was overcast, so Cyril did not have to squint as he raised his eyes to the faraway battlements, beholding the rippling flags in the stiff breeze. He was so engrossed in his thoughts that he did not hear Demetrios' words at first, and his secretary had to tug on Cyril's sleeve to get his attention.

"Your All-holiness!" Demetrios barked to be heard above the wind.

Cyril's mind turned to the present. "Yes, Demetrios. I am sorry. I was merely saddened by what we just endured, and now I am equally suspicious about what lies ahead."

Demetrios' nervous expression gave way to a much sadder one. "Patriarch, I am so sorry for what you have endured," he replied, "not just this week, but for all the time you have graced this city."

Cyril raised his hand as they walked down the street, their descent down the Golden Horn making the journey less arduous. "Christ gives me strength to endure, my friend." He looked toward the sea. "I will admit, however, that to be as faithful as I can in the face of opposition is one thing. To have my opponents from among my own people be so unwilling to understand my convictions is another. I don't even ask they accept my teachings to the full. Just listen to me. But alas, no."

"And now the summons to see Sultan Murad," Demetrios muttered. "Given what some were saying in the church, I would be suspicious of what you might face."

"I face these matters, my good Demetrios," replied Cyril, "as one adorned by the blessings of the Lamb of God, who loved me and gave his life for me. And that love follows me into whatever fire or deep water I might enter." He continued walking, head bowed, thinking back to the verbal storm just days before, when suddenly he saw two soldiers approaching, scimitars in hand.

The lamps glowed steadily in the nave of the church, the light brightened by the icons and paintings on the iconostasis[3] wall to Cyril's right. So dazzling was the radiance in contrast with the encroaching darkness of twilight that the eastern end twinkled like thousands of jewels. *Worship the Lord in the beauty of His holiness,* thought Cyril as the twenty-ninth Psalm came to mind. He ruefully wondered how much longer he would go on worshiping his Lord within these walls.

"Your All-holiness," came the voice of Parthenius, seated directly across from him within the array of other bishops, "may we begin? A number of us have travelled from some distance and are somewhat weary, and I am sure you require some rest, as well."

"Indeed," Cyril nodded. He was quite glad for Parthenius' guiding hand amongst the bishops, for while Parthenius was not in agreement with Cyril's beliefs and actions

3. An iconostasis, in Eastern Orthodoxy, is a wall near the east end of a church's interior, filled with icons and religious artwork of holy people in the Bible and church history. This wall separates the congregation from the area where the clergy prepare the Eucharist (Holy Communion).

amongst the churches in the East, both men personally liked and respected each other, and that relational warmth could go quite a way in what might end up being a tense discussion. "Shall we pray?"

They all rose and Cyril spoke the first prayer. "O gladsome Light of the holy glory of the immortal Father, the heavenly, the holy blessed, Jesus Christ. Now that we are come to the setting of the sun and behold the light of evening, we sing to Thee: Father, Son and Holy Spirit, God. It is good and right that at all times Thou shouldst be magnified, O Son of God and Giver of life: wherefore, the whole world glorifieth Thee."[4]

The bishops stirred from their reverent pose and seated themselves. Cyril nodded to Parthenius to stand and said, "This is indeed a solemn night, but time is of the essence. If you have something to raise for discussion, let us do so with all speed."

Parthenius began. "Your All-holiness, we who stand here tonight in the name of the Holy Trinity, desire nothing more than the good of our Church, the glory of our Heavenly King, and the standing of your blessed soul. What we bring before you tonight is an array of questions."

"Charges, Parthenius!" spat a swarthy, black-robed man two seats away.

Parthenius paused, but rather than wheeling around and responding in kind, he slowly turned and calmly spoke. "You are speaking out of turn, respected Contari. You may be bishop of Aleppo, but here you are one among equals." Turning back to Cyril, but still directing his words at the interjecting bishop, Parthenius said, "And these are questions, not charges."

"Continue, good Parthenius," Cyril replied, keeping a steady eye on Contari.

4. This is a close translation of the Phos Hilaron, an evening prayer known in English as "O Gladsome Light".

"We gather here this evening to pose several inquiries of concern about your teaching as our Ecumenical Patriarch," said Parthenius. "We have been vexed by many of your statements in the confession of faith that you wrote nine years ago, which we have asked for you to clarify."

"The confession which you had printed in Geneva, Switzerland, of all places," groused Theophanes of Jerusalem.

"Good bishop, could you let Parthenius have the floor, rather than bring your own charges against me?" Cyril responded. "At least I have never used relics and the sale of a whole church structure to fend off the loss of a monastery under my watch."

The answer stung Theophanes, who clearly did not want to speak about his failures. "We are here to speak about you."

"And which questions shall we entertain?" asked Cyril.

"The first is your view on Scripture and the Church, O Patriarch," Parthenius stated. "And while no one begrudges you for publishing a document in Geneva, we do have to ask why you dismiss the Church's authority and tradition and set both below Holy Scripture when both are equal."

"I do not dismiss authority or tradition of the Church, good Parthenius," Cyril said, his hands gripping the armrests of his archbishop throne. "I simply say that we believe the authority of Holy Scripture to be above the authority of the Church. This is merely because the Church is led by men, who can sin and commit error. Scripture is given by the Holy Spirit, who cannot sin or commit error."

"So, you say our interpretation of Scripture is deficient?" Contari yelled.

"Peace, bishop!" Parthenius growled.

"I say no such thing," Cyril said, the calm in his voice at odds with his thumping heart. "We can err. I do not mean we will always do so. And we have a great tradition of how we have viewed the Word of Christ and taught it to God's children. I simply mean we must be willing to critique our own understanding. How is that sinful?"

"It sounds more like what the rogues are saying in Germany, Switzerland, and England!" said another bishop.

"But Patriarch," Parthenius said as gently as he could, "this could lead to a more immediate matter of deep consternation, and that is your translation of Holy Scripture."

"Indeed," Contari barked, "for Scripture is not a child's toy to be played with, but a holy revelation from the Triune God. Your work—if it was ever to be done—should have been blessed by a council of bishops rather than be your independent pursuit."

"Again, you are wrong, Contari," Cyril replied in a measured but firm tone. "My translation of Holy Scripture is in Greek. Your misgivings seem to be that it is not in the ancient Greek of the time of the apostles! And I have set the Scriptures in the Greek dialect of today because that is what the shopkeeper, the midwife, the builder, the mother all speak. Why shouldn't they be invited to receive the message of God through the Holy Spirit?"

"As if that is what God intends," snarled Contari.

Cyril sighed loudly. "There was an event called Pentecost, wasn't there?" He looked around at the other bishops. "The Holy Spirit enabling the apostles to speak in varied tongues so anyone from any language in Jerusalem that day could receive the Gospel? Look at churches throughout our world! It is obviously God's intent that all the faithful should be able to read the Scriptures in their own languages."

"You are playing with words!" Contari huffed, beating a rolled and sealed parchment into his hand.

"I am not, good Contari," Cyril replied, suddenly disturbed by the sight of the parchment. *Are my eyes deceiving me?* He thought. *That seal looked familiar, even in this light!* He quickly brought his mind back to the debate. "I simply mean to deepen our people's faith. Our creed tells us that 'we' believe! As believers, should we not solidify our people's understanding of the Scriptures by giving them the Word of God they can read clearly? If we believe that, then shouldn't we live out that truth?"

"Might I request we return at another time?" asked Parthenius, clearly drained by the heated debate. "This is getting us nowhere, but the Patriarch deserves calmer heads and hearts receiving his words. May we reconvene here in a few days?"

His words pleased the assembly, and, after a closing prayer, the bishops began to head to the doors of the cathedral and out into the night air. Cyril approached Contari from behind and took him by the arm.

"My good Contari, please, may we speak?" he asked.

Contari slid his parchment under his robe. "Another time, perhaps?" He smiled, not at all a nice smile. "I have some business to attend to."

The rough hands of the soldiers had shoved him into the prison cell. His body crashed to the floor, which hadn't been cleaned in some time. And as the hours passed, Cyril wondered why he had been placed in this cell. With no windows, he couldn't see his hand before his face in the darkness. Sitting up gingerly because of the pain from the soldiers' beatings, Cyril sighed deeply before hearing a deep groan from the other side of the cell.

"Demetrios?" he called out.

"Ugh!" came the reply. "Yes, it is I." A rustling in what had to be straw gave away Demetrios' position. "Are you well, Cyril, in spite of it all?"

"I have just been praying after I woke, so I spent time with my Savior," Cyril replied, "and now I have you with me, so I have human company. There are worse things."

"I fear those worse things must be upon us soon," Demetrios answered. Sliding in Cyril's direction in the gloom, he rasped, "Listen, I overheard two guards talking about you. Evidently, your coming here was a trap."

"A trap?"

"Yes, O Patriarch. You were called to approach the Sultan under false pretenses."

"I was called to the Topkapi by Sultan Murad because he wished to speak with me about the extent of the cathedral's property. Given the city ordinance and Islamic law ..."

"No, Patriarch. Those were the false pretenses. From what I heard, this arrest was arranged by another."

"By whom?" Cyril demanded, his eyes coming into better focus as he could just make out Demetrios' outline in the darkness.

"Does it not strike you as odd that Cyril Contari was there at the cathedral when you were questioned a few days ago?"

"Aside from his tendency to be more aligned with Rome even though he is a Syrian bishop, no."

Demetrios rubbed his eyes. "You know who else has been in the city recently? The Austrian ambassador. The one whom Contari has befriended."

"Yes, but," Cyril then trailed off, when he realized the awful truth. The sealed parchment! It was no ordinary seal, but that of the Austrian court. And Contari had been carrying it! '*I have some business to attend to*,' he had said, thought Cyril.

"Apparently," Demetrios continued, "Contari and the ambassador made league with the Sultan three days ago. You have been accused of plotting with the Cossacks,[5]

5. The Cossacks in this instance were people who lived in the Black Sea region and originated from modern-day Ukraine. They were opportunistic warriors and had attacked Constantinople in 1615 and 1625, the latter invasion forcing Sultan Murad IV to flee his palace.

and from what the guards were saying, the Sultan is unforgiving, and he will not give you a trial."

A torch shone down the hallway of the jail, illuminating their cell. Cyril looked at Demetrios.

"That must mean only one thing," Cyril said.

"And what is that?"

"I am glad I finished the translation of Scripture," the patriarch smiled, "before it was too late."

The two men were led to the dock at San Stephano, quite the walk from the palace, as the Sultan was carried by his servants on his litter. Every once and again, Sultan Murad rubbed his black oiled beard and gave Cyril a look of total disdain. However, Cyril peacefully kept his eyes forward, and they walked to the dock, beholding a ship filled with Janissaries[6]. The captain came forth and stood before Cyril.

"Patriarch," he said to Cyril in a clipped tone. "By order of the Sultan, you are charged to come with us to receive your punishment." He looked at Demetrios. "Servant, you are not permitted to come."

"No!" shouted Demetrios, lunging toward Cyril as if to protect him, but his friend put up his hands and held him at bay.

"This is where we part, Demetrios," Cyril rasped, a look of hope and peace flooding his face. "Our Holy God has more for you to do on earth. Go in peace, my son."

"But what of you, dear Father?" Demetrios began to weep.

Cyril looked at the glaring faces of the Janissaries on the ship. "I have hungered and thirsted after Christ's righteousness all my life. I believe He is soon bringing me to His table to feast forever and ever."

---

6. Janissaries were the household guards of the Sultan's palace in Constantinople, as well as forming part of the elite corps of the Ottoman army.

CYRIL LUCARIS served five times as the Orthodox Patriarch of Constantinople early in the seventeenth century. Born in Crete, he spent time teaching and ministering in Lithuania and Poland, strengthening the Orthodox believers there. Drawn to the Calvinist theology of the Reformation, Cyril carried on friendly correspondence with leaders in Geneva and in the Church of England. He wrote a new confession of faith in 1629 that sought to show common ground between Protestant theology and Orthodoxy, and his translation of the Bible into modern Greek provoked some backlash within his churches. In the end, Cyril was betrayed by Bishop Contari and the Austrian ambassador who convinced Sultan Murad IV that he was plotting against the Ottoman rule of Constantinople. Taken aboard the ship at San Stefano, Cyril was later strangled to death and thrown overboard into the waters. Although constantly dealing with conflict from all sides, Cyril faithfully expressed the clarity of the Reformed faith while heralding the beauty of the Orthodox religion.

JOHN BUNYAN

1661, Bedford, England

The gavel rapped five times upon the desk, each strike louder than the one before. The accused man flinched at each pounding, his body shaking at each successive blow. He looked to the wall at his left, peering at the frost-glazed windows, fruitless in their attempts to keep out the winter cold. Rubbing his hands firmly together for some degree of warmth, he looked back up at the collection of magistrates before him and particularly the one in the center. Serjeant-at-law and lauded barrister John Kelynge fixed him with a particularly icy stare that was even colder than the temperature outside.

"Will the accused rise?" bellowed Kelynge, and John Bunyan raised his weary body from his seat, saying nothing but continuing in silent prayer.

"John Bunyan," continued Kelynge, "you have been brought before us of this Epiphany quarter session[1] and stand accused of lawless preaching and the illegal convening of worship. These actions are in violation of the Conventicle Act of 1593, which designates that one shall not attend services of religious worship outside the parish churches of the Church of England with more than five members not belonging to one's family. You are indicted upon eyewitness testimony that you have preached in these

1. In the British Isles at the time, quarter sessions were local court hearings held four times a year in the seat of each county, for the purpose of hearing cases that were greater than small matters and did not rise to the level of serious crimes. Bunyan's trial occurred at the Epiphany quarter session because the season of Epiphany in the church year occurs in January.

gatherings, encouraged attendance at the same, and show willful disregard to the defense and dignity of the Church of England. How do you make your plea?"

Bunyan gritted his teeth. The reputation of these quarter sessions was extremely low, and now he saw exactly why. The magistrates would speak of eyewitness evidence but would not offer specifics. Many citizens complained about the open and unwarranted bias the accused often faced from their judges. And now he was here to receive his fate from such a body.

"I state that while you might hold me in contempt of the law of the land," he said, "I have done nothing wrong or guilt-stained against the freedom and liberty of the church of Jesus Christ. And so, I am bound to state you have imprisoned me without cause."

"I believe you are entering a plea of not guilty, then?" chortled the clerk of the peace, a corpulent, dough-faced rascal whose quill pen was overwhelmed by his thick, sausage-like fingers.

"As you will," Bunyan quietly said.

Kelynge leaned over the magistrates' table and pressed the tips of his fingers together. His words spilled from his mouth in breaths that could be seen in the chill of the room. "And what say you about any submission to His Majesty's government, that you will refrain from such illegal preaching as declared by law?"

"To that," replied Bunyan, "I find great comfort in the words of the apostle Peter to the chief priests of the Jews. "We ought to obey God rather than men"![2] And there I shall take my stand, whatever you render."

The magistrates recoiled as if punched in their stomachs. Kelynge himself was especially angered. He lived by the rule that no one showed him up in court, and he sought to counter Bunyan's words immediately.

2. Acts 5:29.

"Then hear the judgment of this court, Master Bunyan," he growled. "You have devilishly and perniciously refused to attend divine services in your parish of the Church of England, as required by law. You have deliberately held unlawful meetings and worships in other structures beyond legitimate churches, bringing great disturbance and distraction to the good citizens of this realm. It is the decision of this session to sentence you to three months imprisonment in Bedford Jail as retribution for your conduct. If you persist in your unwillingness to refrain from illegal preaching and if you refuse to attend services in your parish of the Church of England, your sentence will be extended indefinitely. Do you understand the sentence as spoken?"

"I understand it well, Serjeant Kelynge," Bunyan replied calmly. "And I also understand that it is proper for the sentence to come after the assessment of evidence, not the assumption of it."

Kelynge rose from his seat, barely containing his rage. "Your protest is immaterial!" he shouted, "and the judgment of the sessions stands!"

Again, he brought down the gavel with a savage blow louder than the previous ones, with such force that Bunyan was surprised the gavel shaft remained intact. Soldiers drew to either side of him to escort him to his new future in a Bedford jail cell.

The prison cell door creaked open, and the guard nodded for the visitor to enter. "Fifteen minutes, Master Drayton," he grunted, closing the door on him just after he had crossed the threshold.

Blinking in the oddly well-lit prison chamber, the visitor did not have to search through the room to find his friend. "Master Bunyan!" he exclaimed.

"Samuel!" John Bunyan replied, his voice vigorous despite his recent illness. Crossing the room in a few steps, Bunyan clasped his friend's hand in his own, then warmly embraced him. "It is so good of you to come!" Looking around, he located a chair near the window for his guest and moved a stack of papers from the seat. "Please, sit down, and let us talk. This is such an unexpected pleasure!"

"The pleasure for me is seeing that you inhabit a cheerier atmosphere than what I would expect," said Drayton, his eyes sweeping over the room. He was surprised to find books, pens, and papers strewn throughout Bunyan's habitat, along with a mug of tepid coffee on what looked to be a writing desk in the corner. "In spite of your sentence, they seem to have furnished you with a great collection of comforts."

"That, dear Samuel, is the great advantage of Bedford Jail setting the terms of how prisoners are housed. Even the King's courts cannot touch how I am treated. I admit it is wearying and sad to be so far away from my family, but what I wake up to each day provides a measure of goodly comfort." He looked again at his friend. "It does me good to see you, Samuel!"

"I confess much guilt in not having come sooner," Drayton offered. "The term is over at Cambridge and I was determined to gallop here as fast as possible. I had heard of your imprisonment in January, and then that the court extended your time here indefinitely. Now here we are at Christmas, and I am remorseful I have not come to encourage you prior to this!"

"You have your requirements as a tutor at Cambridge, good Samuel," said Bunyan soothingly, "and I have mine here. Besides, I do not know if they would have allowed you to see me in the early days of my imprisonment."

Drayton saw a low table at the end of the cell with a variety of leathers and jutes[3] and pointed in that direction. "You are busy with tasks beyond writing, then?"

3. Jute is a strong shiny fiber, used to make items such as bootlaces and burlap bags.

"Ah, that is how I support my family," said Bunyan. "My wife Elizabeth and my dear, sweet children require my help. And if you grow up to become a tinker, you develop gifts of handcraft well beyond mere metal. So, I have been making bootlaces and have been able to have them sent to market. I earn a small income from that." He stopped, then went on, a sadness etched on his face. "Of course, being here means I am not with them, especially my dear, dear wife. I was in prison when she delivered our child stillborn, and my spirit gnaws within me that I was not physically present in her sorrow."

Drayton remained silent while Bunyan recovered his emotions. Bunyan took a deep breath then said, "But Samuel, that is not why you came. Do you have news of the world outside these walls? Do you wish to know what has occupied me as of late?"

"Those things and more," said Drayton, seating himself at Bunyan's invitation. "I am not certain how quickly rumor spreads from London, but we receive it increasingly at Cambridge. I regret to inform you that from Parliament, we expect an Act of Uniformity to be passed within the next year. I profess much sadness in this respect, John. Although you are a Separatist and I continue with the established Church of England, I always maintain we need the presence of people such as you, John Owen, John Milton, and the like to remain. I wish you all to have the freedom to preach and worship as you do. If you wish to use the Prayer Book[4], you can do so, and if you wish the liberty to establish your own forms of worship, then do so. Surely there is broad space

4. The Prayer Book refers to the Book of Common Prayer of the Church of England. The Act of Uniformity of 1662 would declare that all ministers in the Church of England would have to use the Prayer Book as the official template for worship. In response to this, over two thousand Puritan ministers (whether Presbyterians, Independents, or otherwise; see the Fact File on the Puritans for more definition) were dismissed from the Church of England in what became known as the Great Ejection.

in which to worship freely. But an increasing number within Parliament do not agree, and so this Act has been drafted."

"Who wrote it?" asked Bunyan.

Drayton replied, "John Kelynge himself, the man who put you here, was the one who led that task."

Bunyan shook his head. "That is sad, to be sure, but I am encouraged by the reality that out of struggle and sadness, God brings the reach of His kingdom to greater lengths. The early Christians in Jerusalem were persecuted brutally after Stephen's martyrdom[5], yet God used that to move them beyond Jerusalem to Judea and Samaria and the ends of the earth, in fulfillment of the promise of Jesus. Paul and Barnabas argued sharply over taking Mark on another voyage[6], and yet their separation meant they could preach to more people apart than they could together. God has a rich history of spinning gold from ashes."

Drayton smiled, crossed his legs in the chair, and then pointed to the stack of papers nearby. "Given the time you have, it doesn't surprise me that you have been writing. How is your output?"

"Surprisingly strong," Bunyan replied with a song in his voice, "and friends have offered to take collections from here and have them published. Any time I can be of encouragement and service to my brothers and sisters in Christ, I count that as the greatest blessing."

"What have you written so far?" inquired Drayton.

"Thus far, I thought it important to offer an account of my trial and these days of my imprisonment," Bunyan answered. "And I thought it best to not write that account as a book, but as a series of letters, as a shepherd to his beloved sheep. I also admit to being struck by the Lord's closeness as I began to dwell here in the cell, so I have

5. See Acts 6-7 for the story of Stephen's bold preaching and death.

6. See Acts 15:36-41.

recently had published a poem—a rather lengthy one it was to write—and a friend had it published for me under the title *Profitable Meditations.*"

"And on what did you meditate?" asked Drayton.

"That all that I did in labor, in preaching, as a husband, as a father, has prepared me to suffer in prison for the sake of Christ," declared Bunyan. "Oh, my good Samuel! I admit I do not love being in this cell, but I do love that I am able to suffer in Jesus' name! I do so love the privilege of taking up my cross and blessing the followers of my Shepherd over and over! And I keep finding new things to share and do and write!"

Drayton leaned toward him, curious. "And what would those be?"

"One has been forming within my heart the past month," Bunyan sighed. "It has been one thing to tell of my imprisonment, but in truth, I am not in this cell because I am a good man and my judges evil. I have received visitors here who say, 'Surely you do not deserve such suffering to befall you.' Who would say I deserve the goodness of God? If God had to wait for those who deserve the grace and mercy from His hand, why, He would wait in vain! No, I need to share with others the truth of my hope, my sin that precedes the grace of Almighty God, so others might know that no one is beyond the loving reach of Christ!"

"You are speaking of a self-biography," Drayton uttered.

"And there are so many places I might journey through my tale!" Bunyan said excitedly. "A group of women were sitting near a door here in Bedford when I first arrived, speaking of the wretchedness of their hearts and yet the sure hope they had in Christ, and I wished for such a hope to rest upon my heart, but I could not fathom it! And again, when the words of Luke fell upon my ears, when Jesus said in His parable, 'Compel them to come in, that my house may be filled, and yet there is room.'[7] That there was still room for a miserable sinner like myself was sweet music to my soul! Every time the devil would tempt me to fall away from my sure hope in Christ, God was not lacking to give me strength for every trial. When Satan would accuse me of my sins, my Lord would whisper delectable truth to the recesses of my being from Isaiah, 'I have blotted out, as a thick cloud, thy transgressions, and as a cloud, thy sins. Return unto me, for I have redeemed thee.'[8] Oh, Samuel, the peace given and the grace bestowed to such a one as I! How should I not tell as many as I can of that great Gospel?"

Drayton smiled broadly, "Indeed, my friend. You should tell the world. Where sin inhabited you, grace abounded all the more."

"I have thought almost those exact words from Paul," Bunyan replied. "This is truly grace abounding to the chief of sinners."

"It goes for all of us," said Drayton, "which is why your words would be such encouragements to us. For we are all traveling from our own cities of destruction to the city of Heaven, are we not?"

Bunyan's eyes flashed with joy. "No doubt we are," he gushed, "and I must say, you have given me an idea for another tale!"

The Separatist minister **JOHN BUNYAN** worked as a tinker[9] before and after a stint in the Parliamentary army in the English Civil War. He married a devout woman who was instrumental in his religious conversion, and he began preaching to a group of believers in Bedford that were not associated with the established Church of England. His

7. Luke 14:23.

8. Isaiah 44:22.

9. A tinker was someone who made or repaired items of tin.

passionate preaching strengthened the faith of many, but the restoration of the monarchy meant his preaching was now deemed illegal. Tried in early 1661 and imprisoned, Bunyan spent twelve years in jail at Bedford. There, he never stopped proclaiming the gospel through his gift of writing. His spiritual autobiography *Grace Abounding to the Chief of Sinners* was published during his imprisonment, but he is most known for his classic *The Pilgrim's Progress* (published after his release from prison), an allegory of the Christian life that has been translated into over two hundred languages and remains a beloved classic of Christian literature.

JOHN OWEN

December 1666, Leadenhall Street, London

The snow flurries swirled gently through the air as the shivering man, clad in his overshirt, black cloak, breeches, and low-heeled shoes, caught his hat before the breeze could remove it from his head. The chill was a welcome relief from the stench of charred material that had surrounded John Owen's daily meanderings since September. Even now, however, he could still smell the smoke and ashes in his nostrils. He pushed away the sad thoughts of what these streets had been prior to the blaze that had destroyed so many homes and buildings. As if sensing his musings, his wife Mary slipped her arm through his, following his gaze toward the meeting hall that sat over a hundred yards away.

"Above all else, my husband," Mary said quietly, "I would say we must rejoice that we have a place to worship Almighty God. Many churches and halls felt the wrath of the great flames. We have a place, and Christ has us. In the midst of sadness, we must recall our blessings."

John nodded. "A blessing indeed that this fellowship is new, as well. I do not know what God's plans are for our future, but you are right, dear Mary. We have known much grief, and not merely with this fire. And yet God is good. Half a moment. Here we are."

They turned into the modest building and, after going down a hallway, the Owens both entered a large drawing room where two dozen people stood. John and Mary nodded and began making their way among them. While

Mary broke off to speak to two women, John approached a trio of individuals near a low table by the far wall.

"Anne," John said, extending his hand to Anne Desborough, "I am overjoyed to see you among us today. Please tell me that our prayers for your husband are demonstrating more success."

"I wish I could tell you the best news that he is freed, Mr. Owen," said Anne. Her husband John had served in the Parliamentary Army during the war against the royalists; now with the monarchy restored, he had been imprisoned in the Tower of London. "And although he is not home, messengers occasionally come to our home and tell me several in the king's court are sympathetic to his plight."

"Have faith, Anne," John replied, "for we will continue to pray."

"You'll be in line with us," said Anne, pressing her hand on top of his, "for I know you and your dear Mary both know suffering."

John could not speak; the reminder of the deaths of their many children, all in infancy, still stabbed at his heart. He felt Mary take his hand gently and respond to Anne, "The grace of the Lord is always sufficient even in darkness, as always. Thank you, Anne, and we will continually pray."

As they walked together toward General Fleetwood and his step-daughter Bridget, John sighed deeply and whispered to Mary. "I wish I could perpetually feel that grace, my love. I speak of God's mercies so often to others, and yet I cannot help but experience a tearing of my heart when I think of the loss of our babes over the years."

Mary squeezed her husband's arm. "The Lord has seen fit to give us those little ones, all ten of them, and then for whatever reason take them away. But in their death, they have joined with Christ and see His face. Dear John, think on what they enjoy now, and be encouraged."

John gathered his emotions as they approached their friends. "Charles, Bridget. How blessed we are to have you here after the terror of a fire that makes no sense."

"To gather together to worship Almighty God makes the most sense in difficult days such as now," General Charles Fleetwood replied, his handshake firm and his smile bright. "I am most encouraged that you have taken up this work, John. You have been a dependable minister. I have no doubt that will continue. We all need bracing courage from your preaching to face the days we do."

John nodded his thanks, turning to Bridget, a beautiful fresh-faced sixteen-year-old. "Your presence here, dear Bridget, does all our hearts well. That you pursue the wonders of the Almighty with such vigor gives me much hope."

"If young people such as yourself keep faith in Christ after such loss we have seen," Mary added, "then that bodes well for the future."

"Your words are very kind, both of you," smiled Bridget, who turned to join her stepfather as the assembly began to gather in a larger interior room. Mary hung back with her husband.

"Be faithful as always," she said to John, kissing him on the cheek, "and God will be with you and speak through you."

"What other hope do we have but His grace shown through the blood of Christ?" asked John rhetorically as he followed the crowd into the makeshift church.

Standing together, the small congregation listened intently as John called them to worship from the ninety-sixth Psalm:

> O sing unto the LORD a new song:
> sing unto the LORD, all the earth.
> Sing unto the LORD, bless his name;

shew forth his salvation from day to day.
Declare his glory among the heathen, his wonders among all people.
For the LORD is great, and greatly to be praised:
he is to be feared above all gods.
For all the gods of the nations are idols:
but the LORD made the heavens.
Honor and majesty are before him:
strength and beauty are in his sanctuary.
Give unto the LORD, O ye kindreds of the people,
give unto the LORD glory and strength.
Give unto the LORD the glory due unto his name:
bring an offering, come into his courts.
O worship the LORD in the beauty of holiness: fear before him, all the earth.

Reverently, solemnly, and joyfully, John then led in the prayers. He gave God praise for His mighty works, begged for the needs of the people there and the citizens of London for recovery from the devastating fire, and then closed with a heartfelt request that the Holy Spirit enlighten their minds and hearts to receive the preaching of Scripture wholeheartedly.

"Amen," came the united response from those assembled.

Looking over the congregation, John was filled with joy for their presence and concern for their wellbeing. *They are truly sheep in need of their Good Shepher*d, he thought, following his inner words with words choked with emotion.

"Let us remain standing together as we sing the twenty-third Psalm as our response," he said, and the people went right into the beautiful melody. Their voices soared, and John lifted his voice with the others!

The Lord Himself my Shepherd is,
Who doth me feed and keep;
What can I lack of true and good

while I am His own sheep?
He makes me to lie down and rest
in pastures, tender grass;
He keeps and gently leadeth me
near streams of quietness.
My failing soul He doth restore
and lead in righteous ways;
And all this freely, that His grace
and name may have the praise.
And though my daily walk doth lie
through death's vale, Thou art there;
All being ever cared by Thee,
no evil will I fear.
For in my lowest, darkest state,
the Lord is with me still:
Thy Rod and Staff shall comfort me
and keep me from all ill.
Thy bounty doth my table spread
in presence of my foes;
My head refreshing oil anoints,
my cup still overflows.
Goodness and mercy all my days
shall keep and follow me;
And in the house of God always
my dwelling place shall be."[1]

The image of Christ as their Shepherd stayed with John through the readings from the Old and New Testament, through another prayer—this time to confess their sin—so that by the time he stood in front of his fellow believers to proclaim the Scripture to them, he was visibly overwhelmed by the image of his Savior in his mind. Taking his well-worn Bible in his hands, he placed it on the lectern before him and paged through it to his text.

"I take as my passage today the glorious words of God's Holy Spirit breathed through the apostle Paul in the fifth

1. From a collection of Puritan metrical psalms for singing.

chapter of Romans," John said in a voice that, though tired, exuded confidence and hope. "We have sung of our Lord who is our Shepherd. Now we receive the good reminder of our Lord Jesus Who, as our Shepherd, laid down His life for His sheep, and today I wish to display the effects of the death of our good and gracious Shepherd.

"To the text," he continued. "Therefore being justified by faith, we have peace with God through our Lord Jesus Christ: By whom also we have access by faith into this grace wherein we stand, and rejoice in hope of the glory of God. And not only so, but we glory in tribulations also: knowing that tribulation worketh patience; and patience, experience; and experience, hope: And hope maketh not ashamed, because the love of God is shed abroad in our hearts by the Holy Ghost which is given unto us. For when we were yet without strength, in due time Christ died for the ungodly. For scarcely for a righteous man will one die: yet peradventure for a good man some would even dare to die. But God commendeth his love toward us, in that, while we were yet sinners, Christ died for us. Much more then, being now justified by his blood, we shall be saved from wrath through him. For if, when we were enemies, we were reconciled to God by the death of his Son, much more, being reconciled, we shall be saved by his life. And not only so, but we also joy in God through our Lord Jesus Christ, by whom we have now received the atonement[2]."

With eyes now sparkling, revived by the glory of the words he had read, John went into his sermon. Carefully, he pressed the truth of Christ into his listeners' hearts, demonstrating what moved Paul to write these words to his original hearers. Yet John knew his friends before him required more. So, he began to construct the hope they needed in the midst of their recent great losses.

---

2. Romans 5:1-11.

"It is true, friends, that our Shepherd did not need to die for us, His sheep. Oh, we desperately needed His sacrifice for any hope of redemption from slavery to sin, for any road out of darkness into light! We cannot avoid that. But let us not deceive ourselves into believing that Christ was forced to the Cross. Yes, He was compelled by His merciful heart and submitted to His Father's will. However, we did not deserve to have Him live among us or die on our behalf. Let us keep that reminder before us. We the sheep have received the reality of our Shepherd's sacrifice, but Jesus in no manner owed it to our account.

"But how glorious it is, brothers and sisters, that in the death of our Shepherd, we receive the effect of it in grace overflowing, in gifts abundant, in a redemption that accomplishes beyond all we could deserve or imagine! See what we have been given out of our Shepherd's merciful heart and His shed blood! For through the death of His Shepherd-Son, God has destroyed the war between Him and us and brings us the peace and reconciliation with Him. Recall the apostle's encouraging words, *For if, when we were enemies, we were reconciled to God by the death of his Son, much more, being reconciled, we shall be saved by his life.*[3] And He has not only provided this peace, but He justifies us by His grace! Those are the apostle's initial words of the chapter, that Christ has taken away the guilt of our sins, gaining forgiveness and pardon when we could not gain it ourselves. He wrenches us from the cursed claws of the devil by becoming a curse for us, by offering His body on the Cross in our place. As the apostle states two chapters prior, we have all sinned and fallen short of God's glory—there is no escape from that blanket declaration! —but still God justifies us freely by His grace as His Shepherd-Son bears the wrath as His blood is poured out!"

3. Romans 5:10.

"Mark well, dear children, that our Shepherd does not merely purchase our salvation, but He does not stop purifying us once we are pardoned. In grace, He captures us in spite of who we are, and because of His grace, He refuses to let us remain that way! Tribulation will come, and in the recent blazes through our fair city, it has come to an extent. But through tribulation, we gain patience, experience, and hope. Christ justifies us by His blood and removes our guilt before God, and the Holy Spirit sanctifies us, purging the filth and corruption of our sinfulness. In Hebrews, we find He renews us in the likeness of God and is an over-flowing reservoir supplying grace so that we might live a holy life, transforming our consciences, and delighting us in serving the living God.

"And this death and life of the Shepherd-Son has given us sonship! We who had once taken up weapons of evil and would have scaled the walls of God's holy abode, if we could, are gently pulled into the embrace of our Father, who had sent forth His Son to redeem us so we might receive adoption as His children. Do you see what your Father has set before you? We who were at war with our Father have been embraced, brought to His table, and given the precious name *brother of Christ, sister of Christ.*

"Yet these effects do not end here on earth. They remain until we are housed in heaven, in glory for all time! From the Shepherd-Son, we receive a *personal* grace, in His death we receive a *purchased* grace, and in heaven forevermore, we inhabit a *perpetual* grace. Oh, dear ones, never lay aside this truth: that you will receive your eternal inheritance, even though for many of us our earthly possessions have been lost in London's flame. Yes, we are burdened by loss, but let us trust that our burdens will truly appear lighter when we perceive the surpassing glory that God has purchased for us through Christ and applied by His Holy Spirit and reserved in heaven for you!

"So let us rise and sing psalms. Let us kneel to pray. Let us walk—no, run! —to meet the Lord here at His table. For in the death of Christ, we find the death of sin, so we might glorify our God forevermore!"

They stood as one, sounding forth another psalm after the sermon. John looked at his wife, at Charles, at Bridget, at Anne, and all the others. And they, having lost so much in the months past, were all smiling.

JOHN OWEN became the most recognized theologian in the English Puritan community. Ordained an Anglican deacon, he left the established church in favor of a Nonconformist path. Supportive of the parliamentary army in the English Civil War, he was chosen to preach in Parliament the day following King Charles I's execution and served as chaplain to Oliver Cromwell, who would govern England after the monarchy fell. He served as pastor to the London congregation in Leadenhall Street after the Great Fire of 1666, and his writings are still revered today for their insightful teaching and devotional impact. Among his books are an eight-volume commentary on the Epistle to the Hebrews, *The Mortification of Sin*, and his book on the impact of the Cross known as *The Death of Death in the Death of Christ.*

FACT FILES

The Puritans

Sometimes when one speaks of difficulty in defining a concept, they might say it is "like trying to nail pudding to a wall." There can be a significant frustration when we attempt to speak about the Puritans in church history. How do we define them? What is a Puritan? As you might guess, there is no easy way to do this.

One problem we have is historical in nature. Are we talking about Puritans in the first half of the seventeenth century in England, the second half of the century, or those who ended up in America during it all? Well, we can really speak about all three periods. And what did they believe? That too, is complicated. What we will attempt in this chapter is to demonstrate the various convictions of Puritans, some things Puritans held in common, and then highlight a few key Puritan personalities.[1]

If one speaks of the Puritans in the first half of the seventeenth century, here we find primarily individuals within the Church of England who wished to make the existing church purer (hence "Puritan") and reform it even more closely to what they saw as biblical principles. These were matters of church government, like proposing a shift from bishops having spiritual authority to churches being led by pastors and elders[2]. For others, it was a question of how people worship God. A number of Puritans came to a specific understanding of what is called the regulative principle of worship,

1. We will have covered other Puritans such as John Owen and Oliver Cromwell elsewhere in this volume, so this chapter will give space to other notable leaders.
2. Refer to my previous volume, *Reform: The Church at the Birth of Protestantism,* and the variety between Calvinist/Presbyterian churches and the Anglican/ Church of England. John Calvin proposed spiritual leadership by pastors and elders, whereas Thomas Cranmer advocated the church retain spiritual leadership by bishops.

that only what was commanded in Scripture could be utilized in worship. Some in this group wanted to get away from the order of worship found in the Anglican Book of Common Prayer and instead have the freedom to construct their own liturgies.[3] Others also did not care for specific holy days on the church calendar, such as Easter and Christmas, and saw them as going beyond the command of Scripture. Some believed in singing Psalms exclusively; some didn't even believe in reciting the Lord's Prayer. Although a number wanted to purify the church, there seemed to be little agreement on how that should be done.

In Britain during the second half of the seventeenth century, the twin desires for the freedom to decide church government and worship differently from the Anglican way grew stronger. By this time, Puritans included an array of Presbyterians, Independents, and Separatists[4]. Also, the monarchy was restored in 1660 under Charles II, who purposed to deal with church matters effectively. A compromise on matters of worship and church government could not be reached, and in August 1662, an Act of Uniformity took effect. It declared the Church of England would be a church led by bishops, not pastors and elders, and a revised Book of Common Prayer would be the standard for worship. With that, many Puritans who were unconvinced of these measures left the Church of England and ministered in Presbyterian churches or other independent contexts. A number of other Puritans ended up in America during colonial times, exhibiting a desire for a church that worshiped and followed Christ biblically.

The Puritans were known for many things, but chiefly for their doctrine, their preaching, and their prayers.

---

3. "Liturgy" here would mean an approach to how people worship God publicly. The word is derived from the Greek for "the work of the people."
4. See the footnotes in "Fact File: Christendom and Conflict" for the definitions of "Independents" and "Separatists".

Beginning in July 1643, a number of ministers met at Westminster Abbey in London and over time produced several volumes of organized topics of biblical teaching called the *Westminster Standards.* These included Anglicans, Presbyterians, and Independents who desired to undertake a revision of the Anglican Thirty-Nine Articles of Religion. What the Assembly produced was a staggering output of doctrinal clarity. The ministers drafted a confession of faith (the Westminster Confession), biblical instruction for young people (the Larger and Shorter Catechisms), a manual for worship, and a format for Presbyterian government. The vision for this work was to capture the depth of the doctrine of the Reformation, and the Westminster Standards are still acknowledged for their clarity and scholarly depth.[5]

Puritans were also known for being dedicated preachers. They produced careful organized and (often) lengthy sermons, passionate to explain a Scriptural text thoroughly and root Christian doctrine in it, then specifically apply the teaching to everyday life as much as possible. Their sermons were long, but Puritan ministers did not ramble, instead offering much supporting truth from Scripture for what they preached to their listeners. And the Puritans were devoted to prayer! Submitting to God and opening one's heart and mouth to him were of utmost importance. Believing God to be absolutely sovereign and loving, one could seek the will of God and also place oneself in His tender care to change one's sinful heart each day. A book worth having is *The Valley of Vision,* which is a collection of many Puritan prayers that echo a desire for a devoted relationship with Christ.

Although there were many Puritans during this era, some deserve special mention. **Richard Sibbes** (1577-1635) was an early Puritan who always remained dedicated to the worship

5. Independents revised the Westminster Confession in 1658 with the Savoy Declaration, and Reformed ministers who had more Baptist convictions produced a revised edition of the Westminster Confession, which in 1689 became known as the Baptist Confession.

and authority of the Church of England. The true heartbeat of his everyday theology was to raise up the spiritually hopeless and weary. Although his writings were many, his *The Bruised Reed* and *The Smoking Flax* brought great comfort and hope to people who were struggling in their faith. He also encouraged his readers to remember their strength was in Christ, not their difficulties, when he said, "The winds may toss the ship wherein Christ is, but not overturn it. The waves may dash against the rock, but they only break themselves against it."

Even though he is known primarily for his epic poetry, **John Milton** (1608-1674) was an outspoken Puritan. Although he studied for the Anglican priesthood, he decided against it due to his emerging Puritan convictions. He traveled to the European Continent, where he met many intellectuals, including the astronomer Galileo, and developed his extensive gifts in writing. He gained fame (and opposition) for many pamphlets he wrote in defense of Parliament's cause against King Charles I in the English Civil War. Defending the Rump Parliament, Oliver Cromwell, and the army's fight against the king, Milton argued that Charles was a tyrant who must be dethroned. When the monarchy was restored under Charles II, Milton found himself hunted, his writings burned, and—now totally blind—dependent upon others to write what he dictated. His loss of sight, though, did not prevent him from producing astonishing literature that rivaled Shakespeare in the English world. In 1667, he published his greatest work, the epic poem *Paradise Lost*, expressing the Puritan ideals of sin and salvation through the story of the world's creation, Satan's rebellion, humanity's fall into sin, and the promise of God's redemption. The result is a stunning panorama of loss and hope in well over ten thousand lines of blank verse in iambic pentameter.[6] Milton followed this work up with

6. "Blank verse" means there is no rhyme scheme to the poetry. "Iambic pentameter" is a rhythm measured by five metrical feet of two syllables each for

Paradise Regained in 1671, depicting Jesus' successful response to Satan's temptation in the wilderness. His writings are still highly recognized in the English-speaking world.

Richard Baxter (1615-1691) is possibly the most acknowledged English Puritan leader, and likely the most wide-ranging in his thought. In his youth, he read Sibbes' *A Bruised Reed*, which led him to a sense of call to the ministry. His church was in the area of Worcester, and when the English Civil War broke out, his support for Parliament did not find favor in a royalist region like his, and he was forced to flee. Although he served as a chaplain for Parliament's army, he opposed the king's execution and Oliver Cromwell's ascension to power. He returned to his church and found his views shifting from an Anglican stance to a Non-conformist perspective. His writing output is unparalleled among English Puritans; his collected works would fill anywhere from fifty to seventy book-length volumes. His *Call to the Unconverted* is a true classic of seeking to evangelize the spiritually lost, and his *The Reformed Pastor* is a fruitful volume about the work of a Christian minister. Just as often as he was revered, he had occasional clashes with other Puritans like John Owen, for Baxter's diverse manner of thought expressed views on Jesus' atonement, perseverance in faith, and the distinction between God's Law and the Gospel that some believed to be outside of Puritan territory. Yet there is no doubting Baxter's passion for Christ and burning desire for people to embrace Jesus in saving faith.[7]

The American Puritans were just as dedicated to spiritual liveliness, and several leaders in colonial times showed a clear vision for government, spiritual direction, and education. **Thomas Hooker** (1586-1647) established a Puritan

---

ten syllables total per line. The cadence of the poetry goes much like a human heartbeat: da-DUM, da-DUM, da-DUM, da-DUM, da-DUM.

7. Other English Puritans include John Flavel (1630-1691), who wrote The *Methods of Grace*, and Matthew Henry (1662-1714), a Presbyterian pastor who wrote a six-volume commentary on the entire Bible.

congregation in Connecticut and founded the capital city of Hartford. He even assisted in writing the constitution for the Connecticut colony. **Increase Mather** (1639-1723) arrived in America after Charles II gained the English throne and began pastoring North Church in Boston in 1664. His keen interest in education led to his being named president at Harvard University (then College), where he served from 1684-1701. Increase's son **Cotton Mather** (1663-1728) was known for his fierce defense of traditional Puritan beliefs. Alarmed at the decline of Puritan influence in daily life and the government structures in Massachusetts, Cotton supported the infamous Salem Witch Trials of 1692. In a stern, yet somewhat frenzied, atmosphere where over two hundred people were accused of witchcraft, he oversaw the condemnation and execution of nineteen people (fourteen women and five men were hung). The trials became a severe blotch on Cotton's character, and his later interests in science were much better received than his intervention in trials. His role in studying and promoting inoculation for smallpox helped him gain entrance into the Royal Society in London in 1713.

As one can see, to define the Puritans as a unified group is a difficult—if not impossible—task. And we can see that Puritan leaders were people of great intellect and noticeable flaws.[8] Mather's *The Great Works of Christ in America* was also a rich resource of New England church history in the seventeenth century. But the commitment to biblical doctrine, careful preaching, humble prayer, and vital education is a legacy that continues to positively affect Christian communities today. If you benefit from a church, a pastor, or a mentor who explains Scripture well and exemplifies prayer diligently, count yourself blessed! These are echoes of Puritan whispers down through the ages.

---

8. However, just remember: Whom else does God have to carry out His mission in the world other than sinful people?

JONATHAN EDWARDS

June 19, 1750, Northampton, Massachusetts

He could hear the babbling of the Connecticut River in the background, but the sound that arrested Jonathan Edwards' attention was the bell ringing at First Church in the center of town. The sweet sound of those peals had initially given his heart a great lurch. His spirit was at variance to any melody playing at the moment. But within seconds, Edwards ignored the frustration he felt. The bells did not know what awaited him today. They could not be blamed. *In truth,* he told himself, *I wonder who could be? So many moments, events, and people have been part of the journey toward this day.* He stopped, then reminded himself, *Including me,* before trudging on.

He approached the steps of the meeting-house and took a moment to look upward. He was especially proud of this church building. Built only a few years after he became pastor, it had three entrances, a generous array of windows for natural light, and the breathtaking steeple over the front steps. It contained a belfry to accommodate the bell and a rooster weather vane at the top that was a personal favorite of Edwards'. *How many times have I preached here,* he thought. *How many years have I labored to bring the light of God's Word to these dear people. And now a council will decide if there is reason for that to continue.* He entered the church and removed his hat as he beheld the people before him and saw the first individual draw himself to full height and approach him.

"Reverend Edwards, it has been quite some time," said Robert Breck, offering his hand to Edwards. "I am sorry we must meet again in difficult circumstances," he continued, then dropping his voice, "but I hope you know the past will stay in the past."

"Where else can it remain?" Edwards responded shaking Breck's hand, his eyes cordial yet wary. The years that had passed had likely done nothing to cool the heated rhetoric that had passed between them at one point. "I have a tribunal to attend and you have work to do on it. Let's leave that in the hands of God."

"I believe that's a favorite line of yours, Jonathan," quipped Breck, offering a sly smile.

"It is a favorite of mine," Edwards replied, "because it is true. Everything, be it our breath, our eating and drinking, and the ability to receive Christ by faith for our salvation, comes from the hand of God and nowhere else."

"We are really going to do this now?" Breck responded. "You have a council to face. I think bantering the fine points of theology is hardly called for now."

"This day is all about that," said another man, approaching the two of them, and gesturing that Edwards join them at the front of the church. "But it will be on our terms and must reach a sensible conclusion. Reverend Edwards, if you will follow me."

"So you are the moderator," Edwards sighed to the seasoned deacon Ebenezer Pomeroy. "I'll pray for the work before you."

"Pray for the work before your own self," Pomeroy said stiffly as they reached Edwards' chair, set behind a sturdy table, "as you should require it."

Jonathan Edwards placed his hat on the table and eased into his seat before looking up at the man who had given him so many recent battles. "Judgment comes at the end of the trial, not prior, my good man. Please try to remember that."

Nineteen men, representing nearby churches, with two men from First Church included, looked down upon

Edwards during the proceedings. As he sat in the front pew of the church, Edwards' first thought was, *So, this is what it is like to sit in the shadow of the pulpit.* All his years of preaching, and he still relished gaining a fresh understanding of the listener's perspective. That thought was immediately followed by a more chilling one, *And I might not have any more sermons to preach here.*

"Reverend Edwards," came the clipped voice of Ebenezer Pomeroy. "You are here before this council, drawn both from your pastoral peers and church members from the surrounding area, to answer an inquiry regarding your teachings, your submission to Christ's Church, and to your conduct as a minister. At the close of our session, we will render a vote-verdict, which will be for recommendation to the congregation of First Church, Northampton, to proceed however they will. Do you understand?"

Edwards, recognizing Pomeroy's desire to bait him into a spirit of contention, merely sat erect in the pew and nodded. "I do, Deacon Pomeroy," he said calmly. "You made the task today unmistakably clear."

Pomeroy nodded to Breck, who looked up from a collection of notes and stared at Edwards. "Jonathan, we may have our differences in theology, but I want to assure you I see us as brothers in Christ. I hope we can proceed in that spirit."

Again, Edwards refused to fall into the trap. "The best way we can proceed in that spirit," he said in a placid tone, "is to proceed. I assume you would like to begin with a question."

Breck tented his fingers together and leaned forward over the table. "Jonathan, I will assure you I understand the authority of a minister to put forth his own opinion, his strong convictions, even. No one can deny that you feel strongly about who may receive entry into the church as members and who may receive the blessing of baptism and be welcome to the Lord's Supper. My first question has to do with the issue of 'Why now? Why so recently?'"

"Why now?" repeated Edwards.

"Surely you know the history of your own congregation," replied Breck. "Your own grandfather, Solomon Stoddard, put forth and supported the larger congregationalism that welcomes children of all people to be baptized and invites all people to the benefits of the meal at the Lord's Table. He had this practice in place here at First Church, which has become widely practiced in churches throughout this colony, well before your arrival in 1727 when you began laboring alongside Reverend Stoddard. Yet there is no indication of your desire to change the requirements for baptism and the Lord's Supper until eight years ago? If this was such a scandalous policy, then why did you tarry so long before moving to change it?"

Edwards sucked in a gulp of air to calm his nerves before replying. "You and I, Reverend Breck, have differences on the description of this practice. You call it larger congregationalism; I call it what it is: A Half-Way Covenant, one which I believe Scripture would show empties these holy rites of their meaning." He held up his hand as Pomeroy sought to interrupt. "As the pastor of this church, for years I held my peace in the hope that the members within were truly bearing fruit of the Holy Spirit that gave evidence of a repentant life. I also did not wish to exert undue strain upon a fellowship unless there was a need to bring difficult matters to light. I also confess that for much of my time over the first decade of my pastorate here, I was obsessed with preaching the Gospel of Christ so that people would clearly see their need of Him. It is my belief that solid preaching will expose people to the truth of Scripture, and the Holy Spirit—not the captivating remembrance of the preacher's personality—will work in the hearts of the listeners. All through the early years, through the times of revivals that swept through our colony, that has been my endeavor."

"So, what changed?" Ebenezer Pomeroy demanded, waggling a finger in Edwards' direction. "Why when there used to be sweetness and light do we now only have the coarse cobblestones of your present complaints against your parishioners?"

"Ebenezer, please," spoke up Joseph Hawley from the end of the bench. "I may be troubled by Reverend Edwards' stance on membership in our church, but he is surely entitled to respect from this council, not disparaging remarks like that."

Looking at Hawley, Edwards smiled slightly. The man's father had been one of Edwards' opponents years before, and the elder Hawley's tragic death still resonated in the Northampton community. To have Hawley come to his defense gave Edwards a slight amount of hope. Clearing his throat, he replied.

"I simply speak of what I see in the evidence before me. The revivals of yesteryear created a great deal of emotion and religious fervor. But emotion will fade, and what matters will be the substance of one's life. As our Lord said clearly in Matthew's Gospel, 'Wherefore by their fruits ye shall know them.' I have merely drawn attention to the chasm between the emotion of expressed hope and the pattern of everyday life. It is one thing to profess Christ; it is another to be possessed by Christ. For one to bring their child for baptism, for one to approach the table of the Lord, that person must be transformed in heart and renewed in affections by and for Christ Himself!"

"And what would you have, Reverend Edwards?" exclaimed another minister on the other end of the bench. "Churches emptied of people because you set the demands too high? A small cluster of those whom you deemed to be true believers as long as you could draw the confines of that circle? Even your grandfather Stoddard proclaimed fifty years ago that all were welcome to the Lord's Supper—believers and unbelievers—because even the unregenerate would receive some benefit from God for tasting His meal! Why should you go against that?"

"Remember, Jonathan," Robert Breck cautioned as peaceably as he could, "that Satan entered Judas who betrayed Jesus, and even our Lord allowed Judas to sit at table for the Last Supper. Recall Luke's Gospel, after Jesus had distributed the meal. 'Behold, the hand of him that betrayeth me is with me on the table.' You cannot deny that."

"I will not deny the Scriptures, Robert," Edwards began, "but neither will I conclude that Judas actually ate the bread and drank the wine. We are either of the kingdom of Christ or the kingdom of the devil! Do not forget what the apostle Paul said to the Corinthian church! 'Ye cannot partake of the table of the Lord and the table of demons.' Because those who come to the Table 'unworthily eateth and drinketh damnation to himself, not discerning the Lord's body.' Those whom Christ Himself has not received should not receive Him. That line I will not cross!"

"Even though you have already crossed lines and crossed swords with others so publicly in this very church?" Joseph Hawley said, almost sadly. "Six years ago, you learned that several lads in this very parish had been dabbling in what you viewed as sinful reading."

"They had taken a manual for midwives," Edwards corrected him, "and had gathered together behind closed doors to read it and gain personal knowledge of the female body. Even you must admit there are other, more wholesome ways to acquire such knowledge."

"And even you admit," blustered Pomeroy, "that you handled it in the most shameful way possible. You stood in this pulpit and read the names of the lads who did so! And they weren't truly small boys. They were largely twenty-four, twenty-five-years old! Being aimless and spiritually adrift is one thing. To be shamed by one's pastor in such a way is another!"

"There is one other matter," Robert Breck said. "And that is about the spirit of your ministry. None of us doubt your ability to communicate well in this pulpit. Or to wax eloquently in your study at home to those who visit. But you hardly seem to know how to lift the spirits of a man in the streets, or a woman enduring the loss of a child. You explain Scripture, sin, and redemption with a silver tongue. Yet I do wish you could do so more often with tenderness." He paused. "Do you have anything to say in your defense?"

After an even longer silence, Edwards stood and replied. "I know that I can point out failings, faults, and turbulent temper in others. And when I have spoken truly about those matters, I know I have struggled with self-centeredness and being brutally direct, which has not honored the name of Christ. If I had more of a spirit of gentleness," he said as tears formed in his eyes, "I should be greatly mended. And that has to be my earnest prayer for as long as I shall continue to live. And I speak from the pulpit regarding sin because I know I must preach each sermon to myself, confronting myself first and foremost, for the shadow of the Cross must first fall across the territory of my own heart." He gulped, taking his hat in his hands and pressing it to his chest. "I am not a good man preaching to bad people. I am a grievous sinner rescued by Christ preaching to wayward lambs. And I wish us all to find rest in the Shepherd's sheep-pen."

Joseph Hawley clasped his hands together, his eyes boring into Edwards'. "And if this council votes for an immediate separation between you and this congregation? Will you accept it if the church aligns with our recommendation?"

Edwards closed his eyes and prayed. *Release me to follow you, merciful Lord, if that be Your will.* Opening his eyes, he said, "If that is to be, then I will submit. And I will follow Christ my King wherever He shall take me."

Robert Breck stifled a cough and replied, "Then may God have mercy on your soul."

"He already has, Robert," Edwards said, his voice filled with peace and hope. "He already has, to an undeserving sinner like myself."

The American pastor and theologian **JONATHAN EDWARDS** lived at the center of much activity and controversy during his life. His preaching was low-key and monotone because he believed people should not be distracted by speaking quality, and God still used his preaching to ignite a great deal of growth in the Northampton area during his ministry. He preached the sermon "Sinners in the Hands of an Angry God", depicting God's wrath against human rebellion while the same God was merciful and desired people to avoid hell and instead seek the grace of Jesus Christ. His battles against the Half-Way Covenant[1] and increasing opposition in his own church led to the event depicted in this chapter. The council ruled against him by a vote of ten to nine, followed by the church voting by an overwhelming majority that Edwards should leave. Eventually, Edwards became a missionary to Native Americans in Massachusetts before becoming president of Princeton University. Not long after moving to Princeton, he died on March 22, 1758.

1. The Half-Way Covenant was a church membership policy enacted in the mid-seventeenth century in reaction to declining conversions and attendance in Congregational churches (those congregations who are independent and make their own decisions about how things should be done) in Massachusetts. It allowed for parents who had been baptized but were not truly converted to have their children baptized. Later on, Solomon Stoddard stated the privilege of Holy Communion/the Lord's Supper should be extended to the unconverted as well as Christians. There was also a political aspect of the Half-Way Covenant. Only church members were considered citizens and thus were allowed to vote in colonial elections. That is partly what led to the Half-Way Covenant.

FACT FILES

Christendom and Conflict

In the seventeenth century, as Catholics and Protestants occupied Europe, there were considerable conflicts that arose, as one might imagine. While we might wish people of different convictions could find other ways to settle differences, it is important to note that passions ran high among the nations. With religion being such a critical part of human existence, people were willing to defend their beliefs and their right to practice them. Sometimes this led to conflict amongst Christian groups; other times it meant Christians joining together to answer outside threats. The 1600s were not without a significant amount of conflict.

The simmering tensions between Catholic nations and Protestant territories led to the clash known as the Thirty Years' War. Rudolf II, the weak Holy Roman Emperor, oversaw an increasing amount of violence in his realm between Catholics and Protestants. Duke Maximilian of Bavaria sought to make Protestants forcibly convert to Catholicism. In Bohemia, Protestants joined together in greater numbers and a band of them attacked the palace in Prague in May 1618, throwing two royal advisors out of a window.[1] Over the coming years, armies of the Protestant League found it difficult to defeat the larger number of the Catholic forces, and many forced conversions or expulsions followed. It was

1. This event became known as the "Defenestration of Prague". In truth, the advisors were unharmed because they landed on a pile of garbage in the street, but emotions over the event were quite raw, and this moment is viewed as the start of the Thirty Years' War. I am condensing a lot of the history of the Thirty Years' War, but it is a period of history worth knowing. Much of the development of the secular states of Europe—and the many French wars that followed soon afterward—had their beginning with the Peace of Westphalia that ended the Thirty Years' War.

when things looked bleakest for the Protestant cause that **Gustavus Adolphus** (1594-1632) led a series of battles that won back some of the ground lost. Gustavus was the young king of Sweden and, after establishing his rule by ending Danish control over his nation, he invaded Germany. As a dedicated Lutheran, he wished to free the German Protestants from Catholic control. Gustavus' legacy grew in several ways. First, he was a brilliant general who emphasized organization of troops, quicker reloading time of guns, and artillery that could be moved more swiftly. Secondly, his armies treated conquered opponents with respect. The Protestant Swedes never forced Catholics to convert, but rather allowed them to practice their faith. Finally, Gustavus was not about building his own empire, but providing lasting peace. He desired religious tolerance for Protestants and Catholics. His success brought the German Protestants to his side, but the Swedish cause suffered when Gustavus was killed at the Battle of Lutzen in 1632. Sixteen years later, the war ended with a stubborn peace, but Gustavus had distinguished himself with much honor. Although the Thirty Years' War ended with little ground gained on either side, Gustavus' courage and ability had turned the tide at a critical moment and led both Catholics and Protestants to seeking a lasting peace as they grew weary of fighting. His legacy of respect and tolerance continued after the war as nations leaned more in the direction of religious freedom for their subjects.

During the middle of the seventeenth century, England endured a series of conflicts between supporters of the king and those of Parliament, known as the English Civil War.[2] King Charles I of England (reigned 1625-1649) sought to expand the power of his monarchy, even willing to ignore the protests and

2. As you might recall from the chapter on the Puritans, the Westminster Assembly did much of its work during this period of the English Civil War.

legitimate complaints of Parliament. Among Charles' church appointments were men who executed harsh measures against Puritans, including death warrants and bodily mutilations. The Archbishop of Canterbury, William Laud, tried to impose Anglican activity upon the Church of Scotland, which had become overwhelmingly Presbyterian. The Scots revolted against these measures in 1637, and the conflict became a war. Charles then had to ask Parliament for funds to raise an army, but the vocal Puritan members of Parliament refused to give the king what he desired.

At the center of these stormy days arose a member of the House of Commons named **Oliver Cromwell** (1599-1658). Cromwell was a dedicated Puritan, one who read the Bible regularly and believed that every decision he could make—whether in his personal or professional life—must be rooted in the will of God. As Charles gathered his forces—nicknamed the Cavaliers—and Parliament formed military units of its own (called Roundheads), Cromwell assessed the situation and believed that Parliament would need an excellent cavalry to counter Charles' own force. Cromwell's heavy horse troops charged into battle singing psalms and won victory after victory, finally crushing Charles' army at Naseby in June 1645. In the years that followed, Charles tried to negotiate with the Scots, Cromwell's army, and Parliament, making false promises to all of them. Cromwell's men emerged triumphant, captured the king, and arrested or expelled Parliament members not friendly to the army's cause.[3] This new "Rump Parliament" then tried Charles for treason and found him guilty. Fifty-nine members signed the king's death warrant, with Cromwell the third man to place his name

3. This action of marching into Parliament and arresting specific members, many Presbyterian, was technically led by Colonel Thomas Pride, and it became known as "Pride's Purge".

on that document, and a remarkably calm Charles was beheaded on January 30, 1649.

Cromwell's battles did not end with Charles' death.[4] Although the Rump Parliament declared England to be a republic with the monarchy abolished, Cromwell grew weary of the lack of true elections for the people's representation. After conducting efficient and ruthless military campaigns against the threats of the Irish and the Scots, Cromwell dissolved the Rump Parliament. As he and the army held power now, Cromwell was named "Lord Protector" and the army drew up a constitution. As Lord Protector, Cromwell oversaw a period of religious liberty that allowed the Independent[5] and Separatist[6] churches a great deal of freedom. He also encouraged Jews to settle in England. Cromwell's administration was also marked by the frustrated hopes of Presbyterians who never saw the extent of the Westminster Assembly fully established in England. Cromwell also continued to outlaw the Anglican Book of Common Prayer, although many Anglican clergy stubbornly continued to use it in worship and resisted Cromwell's desire to make churches less ornate and plainer. Irish Catholics were even less forgiving toward Cromwell for his wars against Ireland and a number of massacres he carried out against them. And newly-founded groups such as the Quakers found persecution to be an ongoing reality.

In truth, someone who lived in conflict against a previous ruler would naturally not be able to lead in

4. Charles I was the most recent English king to be killed. A number of high church Anglicans (those in the Church of England who value very formal worship and church ritual) believe Charles' execution to be one in which he gave his life because of his devotion to his faith, and so they call him King Charles the Martyr.

5. "Independent" churches in England were those in which each congregation governed its own affairs, with no input from bishops or denominational oversight.

6. "Separatists" were English Protestants who broke away from the established (Anglican) Church of England prior to the English Civil War.

complete calm. Cromwell did not please everyone, and his policies toward some could be overbearing. He was, though, a dedicated if flawed Christian who sought to carry out what he believed was the will of God. Cromwell's time as Lord Protector was brief, as he died in 1658. His son Richard succeeded him, but his weak leadership created conditions that led to the restoration of the monarchy under Charles II in 1660.

Yet another conflict of the seventeenth century involved Christian armies not fighting one another but trying to hold off a completely different threat. For years, the Muslim armies of the Ottoman Empire had attempted conquest in eastern Europe, gaining control of much of the Balkan peninsula as well as Greece. Knowing that the chief city of the Holy Roman Empire was the key to conquering Europe, the Ottomans made several efforts to take Vienna. Although armies from the Holy Roman Empire turned the Ottoman attackers away after a siege in 1529, the Muslim warlords were surrounding Vienna again in 1683. In July 1683 Leopold I, the Holy Roman Emperor, made an appeal for military help within his domain, but when few forces came, Leopold and his court fled Vienna, leaving only thirteen thousand troops to defend the city. With a numeric advantage of nearly fifteen to one, the Ottomans looked certain to gain victory and unprecedented access to a renewed push for European domination. To bring about more chaos and a quicker victory, the Ottomans were digging tunnels under Vienna to bury black powder explosives and set them off. With certain death outside the walls and dwindling food within the city, things looked bleaker than the people of Vienna could have ever imagined on the morning of September 12.

However, unknown to the Ottomans, six days before, the Christian king of Poland, **John III Sobieski**

(1629-1696) joined his warriors with troops of other nations of what was called the Holy League. Meeting at the Danube River twenty miles northwest of Vienna, Sobieski led the united army on to the outskirts of Vienna. Keeping his cavalry unit, the eighteen-thousand-strong Winged Hussars, in reserve, Sobieski waited until troops in Vienna engaged with the attacking Ottomans early morning of the 12th, making slow but steady progress in pushing the front lines away from the city. In the meantime, other Viennese soldiers found the explosives in the underground tunnels and disarmed them. At mid-afternoon, Sobieski led his Winged Hussars[7] thundering down the hills from the nearby forest, the largest cavalry charge in human history. The surprise attack overwhelmed the rear guard of the Ottomans, who found themselves nearly surrounded by Holy League warriors. Sobieski's bravery and the Holy League's combined charge sent the Ottomans into full retreat. The victory led to a sustained campaign that re-took land in Hungary and the Balkans back from the Ottomans. Never again would Vienna be threatened from the East as then. So grateful was Sobieski for God's blessing of victory that he announced, "We came, we saw, but God conquered", and the first action after the battle was to offer worship in St. Stephen's Cathedral in Vienna, giving glory to God for a truly incredible deliverance.

Sobieski reigned for thirteen more years in Poland. He was a patron of science and art, supporting mathematics, astronomy, and poetry, and he was a well-read leader. Yet he is most known for his courage in taking on the Ottoman threat outside Vienna in a time of great peril.

---

7. Also known as the Polish Hussars, these horsemen were adorned with bird feathers on their uniforms (hence, the "winged" nickname) and carried lances, swords, and daggers as part of their weaponry. They would begin with a slow charge in a wide formation, but then pick up speed and draw more tightly as they approached the enemy.

Had he not provided victory that day for the Holy League, the Muslim threat could have penetrated the nations of Europe. It is little wonder that Sobieski was hailed as the "Rescuer of Vienna and Western European civilization".

DAVID BRAINERD

May 1746, Cranbury, New Jersey

"Another post!" called out a sweat-drenched worker, his bronze skin glistening in the sun. Dozens of men milled about, dutifully carrying wood and supplies around the building site with great excitement. One such individual, his hands hardened by callouses and covered with a film of sawdust, lifted several boards and strode toward the door frame that had just taken shape two days ago.

"David!" called out one of the tribesmen, rushing to relieve the weary pastor of some of his load. "You should not carry more than you are able. Here, let me take some of that weight."

"A missionary carries whatever weight Christ places upon him," muttered David Brainerd, dropping the boards before stopping briefly to rub his sore back and shield his eyes from the glare. "And I do not think it right to benefit from a new meetinghouse for our church without putting my own sweat and toil towards it. Do you, Tatamy?"

"That is well put, sir," Tatamy said in perfect English—a sterling example of Brainerd's patient teaching over the past two years. Brainerd knew, though, that once other Lanape tribe members would draw near, Tatamy would deftly start communicating in the Unami dialect. Brainerd sensed this tension and placed his hand on Tatamy's shoulder.

"Tatamy, you have learned much," he said quietly, his other hand wiping the sweat from his brow, "but I am here among your people. I do not wish to make you as I am. It will do better for us to speak Unami as much as we can."

Tatamy nodded his agreement as they both picked up the boards and trudged to the meetinghouse area. The opportunity to build a house of worship had energized the tribe more than Brainerd had ever dreamed. He and Tatamy walked into the interior and arranged the boards on the ground to prepare them before they would become part of the floor.

"One year ago," Tatamy marveled, "you could only count me as a follower among the people here. Now we are well over ten dozen because of the work of the Holy Spirit through you."

"The truth that God works through a broken vessel such as myself is both thrilling and befuddling," Brainerd uttered. "I never would have imagined this sight would have been possible."

"Never imagined it five years ago?" Tatamy asked.

"I was about to say I couldn't imagine it five weeks ago," Brainerd replied, the strength in his arms and legs beginning to give way, "but here we are, having moved from Crossweeksung to Cranbury because God in his grace has seen fit to bless us with receptive hearts to his Gospel." He felt his knees buckle and put up a hand. "I am sorry, Tatamy, but I wonder if I am becoming faint."

"You must listen to my voice if you will not listen to God's," came the deep-chested volley from the towering chief who approached both men, "and I think it is not boasting to say each voice gives the same message: You must rest, my friend, or I will force you to take to your bed."

Brainerd opened his mouth as if to argue with Chief Maan'agreet but thought better of it. Smiling instead, he replied, "Seeing that you could render me unconscious with one strike of your hand, I will relent, O Maan'agreet. But I still do not relent of my desire to see this project to the end ."

"Rest now, help later," Maan'agreet kindly told him, "and to ensure you stay away and take your rest, I assign Tatamy to stand guard over you." He nodded kindly to both of them before turning back to oversee the laborers.

"It is remarkable that Maan'agreet takes such an interest in the building of the church," said Brainerd as he took a bite of bread from the satchel Tatamy had brought. The two men sat down on the banks of the brook, about a quarter-mile from where the rest of the workers labored on.

"It is his way," Tatamy mused. "Some chiefs among the Lanape clans would not be in the midst of the workers. Maan'agreet has come to love Jesus. He believes he must love the work that goes on for Jesus. Being a part of this building is consistent with his love for Jesus. We are blessed to have him." Tatamy paused. "As we are to have you, David. We cannot imagine being without you."

Brainerd had a far-away look in his eye, with such a dour look on his face that Tatamy asked. "Is something wrong?"

"No," said Brainerd, leaning back on his elbows. "At least nothing more than usual, Tatamy. I am merely so exhausted that sometimes I wonder how much time I have remaining with your tribe. It is a wonder things have proceeded as they have."

"This isn't like you, David," Tatamy said, bewildered, "and I've known you to have some significant trials among us. You had to be patient before many of us believed, but that happened. Remember just nine months ago when you preached at Crossweeksung and the power of God came down upon our little group, and sixty-five praised Christ that afternoon? Remember how those from tribes all around have come to hear you preach?"

"Yes," Brainerd said, temporarily cheered, "and had it not been for a few prior differences, I never would have had this chance."

Tatamy now grew wary yet curious. "Go on. What differences do you speak of?"

Brainerd took a drink of water to force down the dry bread. "You have been my good friend for the past year, Tatamy, and I chastise myself that I have not told you or your wife of this before. Less than five years ago, I was set to enter my third year at Yale University."

"The school in Connecticut?"

"In New Haven, yes. A fine school it is, too," Brainerd said, the pain of the memory slicing his heart. "I was studying and receiving fine marks, and I felt the Lord had called me to be forever devoted to his service. During my second year at Yale, two men, George Whitefield and Gilbert Tennent, had come to New Haven and preached forcefully and lit a flame of passion within Yale. I had been gravely ill not long before and so the thought of doing magnificent things for Christ with what life I might have remaining appealed greatly to me. I would often visit fellow students, teach them and pray with them, and was very zealous for the kingdom of God. Looking back, that zeal erupted in unhealthy ways. Reverend Tennant had preached on the dangers of ministers who might seem outwardly godly but inwardly were far from the cross of Christ. When I returned for my third year, there was a new rule afoot: No student could comment, either specifically or by implication, that the chaplain, trustees, or professors were un-Christian men. If one would do that, he would need to publicly confess his breach of the rule, and a second offense would be cause for expulsion from Yale."

Tatamy saw where this was leading. "You have said before that you have not received a university degree. Was this the reason?"

"It was. Now, I had not said anything brazen or openly about anyone. My offense came in a private conversation that I had about one of our tutors. My zeal got the better of me and, not seeing much fruit of the Spirit in this man's life, I commented to my friend that the tutor had no more grace than the chair upon which I sat. Well, a first-year student overheard the conversation and reported my words to another tutor. In consideration, I had made that remark based on one time the man prayed aloud and I judged the prayer to be lacking in substance. I should have restrained my words, but I refused to confess my fault, and the powers that be at Yale expelled me just four years ago."

"And your work up to that point," Tatamy exclaimed, "was for naught?"

"I was aghast over my behavior," Brainerd said, staring at the creek as the memory forced the tears from his eyes. "I sought forgiveness from the tutor. I wrote out a lengthy confession of my fault. Others begged that I be reinstated as a student. But the rule was set in stone and perhaps they believed they must set an example. I can't blame them. It was quite a stupid decision on my part."

"It must have been a very sad time for you," Tatamy agreed, shifting his position in the grass, "but the words of Joseph come to mind. *What you meant for evil, God caused for good.* If you had remained at Yale, your path might have been directed elsewhere than among us."

"Yes," Brainerd replied, allowing a smile, "that extraordinary providence of God is the bright light against the darkness of that expulsion. Had I continued on at Yale, I might have been ordained to the ministry. I might be laboring somewhere in a corner of God's kingdom. But it would not have been this corner with you and the rest of the Lanapes. And I will add this: That experience humbled me. It broke me in a way that was necessary and proper. It caused me to hate my sin all the more. I came to see that I needed to treat everyone as if seeing them through the eyes of Christ and not my own."

"I do not doubt you have learned from the past," Tatamy offered, "and it does not surprise me. My people have long said the past is the greatest teacher when we are willing to be its students. As for me, I am glad you have come to dwell among us."

Brainerd looked pensively at the sky, then at his friend. "I am, too. I admit I have struggled to love others well because I am anxious over my circumstances. I have been offered opportunities elsewhere." He waved off Tatamy's look of surprise. "Oh, don't worry. I am not going away. I mean to say there were times I was given the chance to be in a quieter environment, a more settled life. One was near my hometown of Haddam, back in Connecticut. Another was on Long Island. Anyone might think those were idyllic places, and to many they would be."

"Then what made you stay?" asked Tatamy.

Brainerd looked off in the middle distance. "Very often, I truly believe that when the Lord sets two paths before you, one more difficult than the other, it seems the path with more trials, and difficulties is where He desires that you walk. I cannot explain it. I do not pretend I enjoy life's hardships. But it is more important to be faithful to the Giver than merely enjoy His gifts."

"To your credit, David ," Tatamy replied, "I do not see you wavering there. Oh, I have seen you sad. I have seen you in your most downcast moments. But God does not let go of you."

"That is what I find unfathomable, good brother," Brainerd sighed. "I remember preaching to your tribespeople and feeling the Lord filling my heart with compassion for them, and then I felt such great sadness that I could not feel more. I have suffered great guilt because I prayed for the Lenape and fallen asleep, wishing that I could avoid rest to pray more. I can barely get out of bed each morning because of the challenges before me, and yet my greatest anxiety is that I cannot do more. It is so distressing to feel within me the corruption of sin that remains. I do not believe myself to be worthy of a place amongst your people. Sometimes, I am so greatly dejected that I don't know how to live. And I wish I could love others as well as God has loved me. All I can say is that I can be glad His grace, not my endeavors, is what sustains me."

Tatamy reached over and touched Brainerd gently on the shoulder, the tender clasp that offered so much between brothers in Jesus Christ.

"Dearest David," he said, "no one could have done more among us than you. And there is no one I know who has suffered more for another people than you. I just plead with you to remember that long after you are gone from here Jesus will stay, because you have planted him among us. He will remain with you wherever you go."

"Long after I am gone, you say," Brainerd said before sputtering a cough. "That might come sooner than we imagine." He slowly picked himself up from the ground as Tatamy joined him in walking back to the building site, hearing a commotion among the men. "I woke up coughing blood today. I hope it isn't the sign of something more dire." He paused again. "Although if God wishes to call me home, His will be done."

"His will seems to be done in a magnificent way before us!" exclaimed Tatamy, pointing ahead to the frame of the church as Maan'agreet approached them.

"How good you came back now!" smiled the chief, taking Brainerd by the arm and waving his own arm toward the skeleton of the church. "For now we can show you Who you have brought among us."

Brainerd looked through the haze of the setting sun toward the church when he saw it. There, resting against the door frame, was a large, carved wooden cross, ready for mounting when the church was fully built.

Grinning from ear to ear, Brainerd allowed the tears to flow freely. "I have been able to do so, dear chief," he said, "because Christ has brought Himself to me." He closed his eyes and prayed. *Always keep me near you, Lord Jesus, near Your cross, near Your very self. Always be my dearest hope.*

The short, twenty-nine-year life of **DAVID BRAINERD** was one of diligence and service to Christ. In spite of his dismissal from Yale University, Brainerd caught the attention of Presbyterian minister Jonathan Dickinson, who encouraged him to consider missionary work among the Native Americans in the colonies. Working among the Lenape tribe in Pennsylvania in 1743, he soon moved to New Jersey and, in spite of many discouragements and his own bouts with depression, his ministry among the Lenapes there bore much fruit as many became believers in Christ. His work slowed as he was overcome with incurable tuberculosis, and he spent his final days being nursed by Jonathan Edwards' daughter Jerusha. On October 9, 1747, Brainerd died and entered into the presence of his Savior Jesus whom he knew to be his only hope.

GEORGE WHITEFIELD

September 29, 1770, Newburyport, Massachusetts

It was a glorious early autumn day, which did not surprise Jonathan Parsons at all. The pastor of the Old South Presbyterian Church was fond of saying that "September is one fine month to be outdoors in New England", and the weather was not disappointing him or the townspeople. Occasionally Parsons would feel the aches of his sixty-four years in his bones, but the cooler atmosphere and shining sun brought vigor to his heart. And giving his face a broad smile was the presence of his approaching friend who was drawing near the parsonage.

"I apologize for imposing upon you for lodging," said his friend, "and for being late today. I dismounted the horse-cart a half-mile away because I thought the walk would do me good."

"It appears it has, my brother," said Parsons, giving George Whitefield a hearty embrace. "No need to apologize, although I am concerned with those stooped shoulders and that slight wheeze."

"Bear that no mind, Jonathan," Whitefield replied, waving his hand dismissively and placing his travel case on the parsonage steps. "As I have told so many on this excursion to America, I would rather wear out than rust out." He looked up at the sky and around at the leaves that bore the creeping touches of yellow, orange, and crimson. "And I'd rather spend it here than in the crowded streets of Boston for now. This country and ocean air blesses my lungs more than I can say."

"We'll have dinner prepared for you in a couple hours," Parsons smiled, "but perhaps if you wish to leave your case here, we can go for a walk."

"I'll follow your lead, Jonathan," said Whitefield, placing his hand on Parsons' arm.

Their stroll led them to Oak Hill, a five-minute walk southwest from the church, and it was obvious to Parsons that Whitefield was more dependent upon him for physical support. "I have to say, it is good you to welcome me to your home, Jonathan," Whitefield said.

"And why shouldn't I?" Parsons replied. "The work you have done on the Lord's behalf here in America? The countless souls who have received the new birth in Christ through the directness and passion of your preaching? Why should my offering you lodging be so special?"

"I am so weary," Whitefield said before enduring a brief coughing spasm. "And when one becomes weary, the tiring nature of each day forces one to take stock of life. I have been thinking back on my days, even as I trudge on and get closer to the day when Jesus receives me into heaven, I become more aware of my failings here on earth."

"We all have failings," Parsons quipped. "Sin has gripped all of us, whether one is a mindless drunk or a conscientious saint."

"I sense many days when I stand closer to the mindless one than the saintly one" said Whitefield. "I have thought more of it since Elizabeth died. I once said I believed that if God would give me a wife then I could live contentedly. What I meant was that a wife would not interfere with my travels and preaching. I now see that my expectations brought me great unhappiness. I was not as tender with her as I should have been. She even told me she believed she was a burden to me." He walked on beside his friend. "I feel great guilt about her passing. I have valued my preaching more than her. I must confess my blame in that. And if that is the case, why would anyone wish to hear a message from God through me?"

Parsons slowed the pace of their walk. "I could counsel you in how to live after her death, but I doubt I would be helpful. Still, you should consider this: Who else can preach to sinful people except for sinners? Who else can Christ send?"

Whitefield still looked pensive. "It is more than that, but I should speak of those things after the evening meal. I am ruining this time together with my memories."

The evangelist's breathing became deeper and more guttural, and Parsons nearly suggested turning back to the parsonage when they reached the field adjoining Oak Hill to elated shouts from a crowd of people there.

"Reverend Whitefield, you're back!" cried one man.

"I can't believe you have returned," called a woman. "Oh, we had prayed we could see you again!"

"It's him!" said a young boy excitedly. "Reverend Whitefield! You, sir! Your preaching changed my father and got him off drink and now he says Jesus saved him because of your words!"

Parsons was determined to keep Whitefield's strength up and the crowd at bay, but when he saw Whitefield himself rise to his full health, the color return to his cheeks, and the light shine in his eyes once more – this was the George Whitefield he remembered! This was the man who preached to hundreds, thousands ... his words reaching into hearts and souls and causing rough men, kindhearted ladies, and little children alike to weep openly over conviction of their sin and the offer of eternal life in Christ! The people clamored around Whitefield for several minutes, plying him with questions and memories, until at last, the evangelist spoke up.

"Well, Reverend Parsons, it appears the Holy Spirit has gone before us and provided the tonic I need. These people have greatly lifted my soul, and perhaps I can show my gratitude by addressing them."

"Here in the field?" chuckled the incredulous Parsons.

"If I have a platform upon which to stand, then I can see everyone," Whitefield replied as the crowd of over a hundred gathered around.

"Got just the thing," shouted a man on the edge of the assembly, rolling a barrel toward Whitefield. "Use this to stand on. We can help you with the step up."

Whitefield nodded, his eyes shining as he blinked back tears. The people watched him slowly ascend the top of the barrel and then gaze upon them. And there, from the top of a barrel in the middle of a Massachusetts field, George Whitefield began to preach.

The sermon began, as so many before, with the reminder that they were drawing near to the face of God, sinful people, and Whitefield asked they bring broken and soft hearts before a holy God. Parsons bowed his head. *He is speaking to himself as much as to them, he thought. He is seeking the mercy of God along with them. He is preaching to himself.*

For over an hour, Whitefield went on, his hands rhythmically dancing in the air with every gesture. From memory, he recited Scripture after Scripture, demonstrating the sinfulness of humanity before moving into the heart of the Gospel, leading his listeners to the feet of Christ. Parsons looked around as Whitefield spoke eloquently, fervently, of the suffering of Jesus that opened the way of life for the wretched.

"We think of our sins having nailed him to that cross," Whitefield thundered, the pain in his lungs causing him to sway on the barrel, "and so they do, but let us not watch him suffer from afar, from this field in Newburyport, as if he was many years and half a world away! No, you are there at Calvary. I am there at Calvary! Our voices call out among the mockers and scoffers until our throats are hoarse. We lose our voices! We defend our sins! And then we realize that we have no hope except in that suffering Messiah. We would die except for Jesus, who died that we might live. And so we drift past the shrieking Pharisees, past the Roman guards, as if they cannot see us, and we stand at the foot of that cross. Do you not, my dear friends, see yourself standing there?"

He paused for effect, and Parsons saw the image of his friend on the barrel grow blurry. And it was then that Parsons recognized he was, in fact, weeping. Whitefield went on.

"You cannot stop yourself, can you? You reach up and take hold of that cross. You touch the rough wood and feel the blood coursing down the cross, and you believe ... you know for certain that this man, God the Son, Jesus Christ, the King of Kings, is your only hope for new life, for life eternal with him forevermore.

"You can cast all else aside. You must cast all else aside. I must cast all else aside! What indeed have we brought that can force the hand of God to save us, but nothing! We say, our works? Works? Works? As if we could get to heaven by works! I would rather think of climbing to the moon on a rope of sand! Let not another moment pass by if that is not the cry of your heart this day, where you place yourself in the arms of Christ, and by faith in his blood, shed for you...in his very self, risen for you, and receive his new life offered to you in the Gospel!"

Parsons stood admiringly on the edge of the crowd. His friend could still preach. He could still bring people to the Cross as if they were on the outskirts of Jerusalem itself. What an incredibly legacy.

Parsons sat down at the dinner table with Whitefield, the delicious supper of roast chicken, beans, and bread finished. He had just helped Phoebe clear the dishes and would have helped her with the washing up had his wife not shooed him away.

"Don't ignore your friend, husband," she smiled wearily, rubbing her aching hands and stepping toward the stairs painfully. "You have some catching up to do and I can just let those soak until the morning. I'll be going to bed. Reverend Whitefield," she addressed the evangelist, "I apologize for being such a poor host, but I feel quite unwell. Perhaps a night's sleep will guide me to services tomorrow."

"You are very kind in feeding me, dear Phoebe," Whitefield said graciously. "I will be taking my rest soon, but I shall enjoy this time with your worthy husband."

Phoebe nodded as she left, and Parsons watched her ascend the stairs to the bedroom. When she was out of earshot, he turned to Whitefield. "She is God's gift and a blessing as a pastor's bride. And as you can likely tell, very ill."

"Is it that bad?" asked Whitefield.

"We cannot discern, and the doctor wonders if it might be her heart," Parsons replied. "I do not expect her to live to the new year." He placed a mug of cider before Whitefield. "But for now, fortify yourself. You are here in America to proclaim God's Word. We've needed you back on these shores."

"I've missed these shores," said Whitefield, "but I wonder how many times I will be blessed to be in

America. I look back on what I have done and it seems such a mixture of joy and sadness. I find myself rejoicing over what God has done through me and yet crestfallen over what I do to impede that."

Parsons hesitated. He had not known Whitefield to be this vulnerable. "This seems an odd turn to our conversation, George. You spoke of your shortcomings as a husband before, but for you to raise these words now makes me imagine there is more on your heart."

Whitefield took a sip of the cider and wiped his eyes. "My life has been filled with so much opposition. Much of it has been good and necessary. The preaching of the Gospel always opposes Satan and all the power of hell. I know that. But I have sometimes directed opposition toward others who did not require it. I attacked the Church of England so much I thought I would be martyred as a response. I always believed that the more I opposed, the more joy I would feel. I went from town to town, drawing people to Christ and absorbing the anger of those who hated true religion but there were times when my desire for controversy blazed forth upon others who bore the name of Christ."

"Is this your quarrel with John Wesley again?" asked Parsons.

"Oh, John! I regret the way in which I confronted him! I preach we are saved due to the free election of God; he places the choice into human hands. But I confess we are truly brothers in Christ. In fact, when we stand at the end in the throne room of Jesus, I would imagine I will be on the outskirts of the crowd of saints and he will be so close to the throne I won't even see him."

"Have you told him this?"

"I have, good Parsons," Whitefield replied. "And we have reconciled after a fashion. I hope to see him again, however unlikely that may be. I wish to be reconciled face to face with so many."

Parsons leaned forward and touched Whitefield's arm. "George, the mark of a minister of the Word is not that he has kept himself spotless, but that he trusts in the spotless Lamb of God, Jesus Christ the Righteous. It is not that he has wronged no one, but that he seeks the forgiveness secured by Christ's blood." He squeezed Whitefield's arm. "Take hold of that, George! You preach of taking hold of the cross and that you take hold of it as well. Grasp Jesus in all his faithfulness to provide cleansing and hope tonight!"

Whitefield was the one weeping now. Several moments went by before he could compose himself to speak. "Thank you, Jonathan," he whispered through tears. "You have driven my preaching back into my heart. And even though my body is worn out, my spirit is joyful." He clasped Parsons' hand. "That might be a good word to end on so I can get some sleep of my own."

"May the Lord grant you the rest he desires to give you," Parsons said warmly. "Morning comes soon."

Whitefield rose from his chair and rubbed the pain in his chest. "That is more true than we might realize," he said, embracing his friend and then walking up the stairs to lie down for the final time in his life.

The evangelist **GEORGE WHITEFIELD**, one of the founders of Methodism, became the most famous traveling preacher of the American Great Awakening (a.k.a. The Evangelical Revival) in the years preceding the Revolutionary War. Born in Gloucester, England, in 1714, Whitefield was part of the "Holy Club" at Oxford with fellow ministers John and Charles Wesley and found great passion for preaching the good news of Jesus Christ. In 1740, he preached a series of meetings that helped launch the First Great Awakening, an outpouring of religious fervor marked by conviction for sin and need for salvation in Jesus Christ. Preaching nearly twenty thousand times to over ten million listeners in America and Great Britain, Whitefield's dramatic appeals to Scripture and new life in Christ convicted many of their need for redemption. He traveled seven times to America, where he died on the morning of September 30, 1770, in Jonathan Parsons' home in Newburyport, Massachusetts.

HARRY HOSIER

May 13, 1781, Fairfax County, Virginia

"Whoa!" came the gentle yet firm command of the driver, and the horses slowed their pace quickly to a crawl, dug in their hooves, and stopped next to the wooden structure. The coachman held the reins firmly with hands both black and strong. Rising from his perch, he took a quick crossover step to his left, alighted to the jump seat, and skipped onto the grass, still slick after last night's rain. At no point did the coachman take his eyes off his horses or his hands from the reins until he tied them securely to the hitching post. Placing his hands on the small of his back, he leaned back and held a stretch for several seconds before exhaling loudly and straightening up. Turning back to the wagon, he scooted toward the jump seat as his minister friend alighted from it.

"Another smooth ride over an unfamiliar highway, good Harry," said the minister, tipping his hat to the driver and clapping him on the shoulder.

"I hold the reins, the horses know what's what, and the Lord's angels direct them onward, Master Asbury," said Harry Hosier, who turned around and looked at the church, where several parishioners were filing in. "We mean to go there today?"

Francis Asbury tucked his Bible under his arm and rubbed his hands slowly, nodding assent to Harry's question. "Indeed, we are. You sound surprised, my friend. You are not dubious about the church itself, are you?"

Harry looked at the weathered sign rooted in the grass on the south side of the church. The words "Adam's Chapel" were etched on the boards, but Harry's scrutiny did him no good. Seeing writing and words made as much sense to him as if someone had told him to swim the Atlantic Ocean. Politely taking off his own cap, he said, "Naw, Master Asbury. Not dubious. Not afraid. It's a good structure. Well-built, from the looks of it, and looks but about a couple years old. I'm just confused about our audience here."

Asbury followed Harry's gaze. Clusters of Black men, women, and children walked down the road toward the church as both men could hear the piping notes of an organ somewhere inside the chapel. Asbury smiled at the reason for Harry's wonderment: For every three slave families, there would be a couple individuals whose color was as doughy as Asbury's own complexion.

"Indeed, Brother Harry," Asbury said in as assuring of a tone as he could muster. "A number of people, both black and white, come here. A number of the Blacks are freedmen, just as you gained your release from slavery. Admittedly, this makes it unique for Virginia, but we take our congregations as they are. Though, your voice betrays that you have questions."

"Many, Master Asbury," Harry uttered. "One being did you know such a crowd would be here? And on what do you intend to preach?"

"Oh, Harry," Asbury replied reassuringly, "let's leave what I knew to the side. And I intend to preach the Word of God applied to the present conflict that we pray will end soon. Come, see. Ah! Dr. Rush, a pleasure to see you, sir!"

An intelligent-looking fellow with a high, sloping forehead and thin nose approached Asbury, extending his hand and giving a warm smile to both him and Harry.

"Reverend Asbury, I give you thanks for letting me know ahead of time that you would be in the area. It is so good to see you again, and I trust this is your traveling companion?"

"Harry Hosier, meet Dr. Benjamin Rush, former physician with the Continental Army and a fine addition to each in any medical college once this war is over!' exclaimed Asbury. "And Dr. Rush, this is Harry Hosier, my coachman, my sympathetic ear, and a sponge that soaks up the water of Holy Scripture when read to him."

Harry was surprised when Rush offered his hand to him. "The reverend is too kind, doctor. I just try to listen well and God's Word stays with me."

"Well, I look forward to hearing from you today, whether it be one or both," said Dr. Rush as he doffed his cap and turned to enter the church. "See you inside!"

Harry watched him go and then whispered to Asbury. "That man was the doctor for the whole army?"

"And represented Pennsylvania at the Continental Congress five years ago and placed his name on the Declaration of Independence," said Asbury, watching the weight of those words impress itself upon Harry. "And he desires the freedom, not just of our colonies from Britain, but of you and all your brothers from the yoke of slavery."

"He does indeed?" marveled Harry.

"And," Asbury replied, his mind working, "he might have given me another idea." They walked into the church as they heard the singing begin.

Even with the windows thrust open as wide as possible, there was hardly a cross-breeze coming through the sanctuary, and the worshipers fanned themselves with their hats and hands as best they could. For his part, Harry was glad to worship after hours of driving the horses on their journey, and as Reverend Asbury mounted the pulpit to preach, Harry joined the other congregants in their seats. Even that was a surprise to Harry, for as he looked around, he saw many of his fellow Blacks seated in the pews closest to the front, while the white men and women huddled toward the back. Separate, he thought, but it is odd that our positions are different this day.

As Reverend Asbury preached from the Gospel of Mark, Harry allowed his mind the indulgence of wandering for several minutes. Even his position—indeed, his very life—was much removed from Asbury's. The preacher was white; he was black. Asbury had left school early in life as he couldn't abide the bullying in his schoolhouse in Snail's Green back in England. Still, he had received something of an education and could at least read and write, which were skills beyond Harry's ability. Asbury was well connected and could charm those he met in no time at all. Harry was more reserved and, truth be told, he felt painfully shy and awkward.

But last year, Asbury decreed to Harry that their meeting and Harry's employment as the preacher's driver and guide had been appointed by the hand and mouth of Almighty God Himself. While Harry did not share that confidence at first, in time he grew to appreciate Asbury's friendly manner over the long wagon rides on the frontier. Their travels often had to skirt battle regions between the English and Americans, and on those long rides, Asbury would take out his Bible and read long portions of Scripture to Harry to pass the time. Harry was heartened that Asbury would read to him. What surprised them both was the day they both realized Harry was absorbing more than either man could have imagined.

"The Lord is a patient one, isn't he, Master Asbury?" asked Harry one evening as they clattered north of Greensboro, the guns exploding within earshot from Guilford Court House to the south of them.

"He is indeed, Harry," replied Asbury, tucking his Bible away after reading about the Israelites grumbling to Moses in the wilderness. "One wonders why He is so patient with His people. They complain so often, forgetting he led them from their bondage to sin."

Harry shifted the reins and pulled back, forcing the horses to shorten their stride on the road's slight decline. "Yes, sir, but I don't mean just in the wilderness. God has been most patient with His children for a long time. I mean, a long time!" he exclaimed, his voice drawing out the last adjective with extraordinary emphasis.

"How do you mean, Harry?" Asbury asked him. "I say, I quite agree with you, but I am sure you have your list of reasons. Is it something you've seen in your own life?"

"My life, yes," Harry replied, easing up on the reins as they reached the base of the hill, "but I was thinking of all the ways the Lord held off on His people when they neglected Him in the very Word you read to me."

"In the Word I read to you?" Asbury's excitement grew.

"Yes, sir, because when you read just now about them complaining about no water and God gave them water from the rock," Harry went on, "I say to myself, 'Well, they'd done that before. They'd forgotten God before.' Not just in the wilderness, Master Asbury. When you were reading from Genesis, and when Father Abraham went down to Egypt in that famine, he lied about wife Sarah being his wife. He said she was his sister, 'cos he didn't trust God to protect him in the shadow of great Pharaoh! And later on, old Father Abraham grew weary of waiting on God's good promise of a son, and when Miss Sarah told him to go on and make a boy with servant Hagar, he did. And Father Abraham listened to his wife and not the promises of the Lord."

"This is so amazing, Harry!" Asbury exclaimed. "You remember that story like it was the most brightly colored painting!"

"Yes, sir. It was Genesis 16, or so you said. It made me sad, 'cos Father Abraham had just met God in that smoking pot the chapter before, and God said he would have the land, and in chapter 17 you read how the Lord promised Father Abraham children more than the sands on the seashore. His promises all over the place, firm as firm can be, and Father Abraham forgot."

"How do you remember that so well, Harry?" sputtered Asbury. "I read through those stories only one time, maybe two, on our travels!"

"Ah, it isn't only Father Abraham who forgot the Lord. Rebekah and Jacob went a-scheming to keep God's promise, like the Lord was so helpless He needed their assistance. Genesis 27, right? Jacob lied that he was his brother to his helpless, blind pa Isaac. Jacob had two wives and neglected Leah. Doesn't seem right to me. Oh, and don't forget Joseph's brothers. Mad as hornets they were over his dreams that they sold him into slavery. That especially made me sad. No, it's not just Father Abraham. God's people have long tendencies," Harry continued, drawing out the word tendencies, "to forget Him. That's why the grumbling in the desert makes me sad. Not that it's so new when they have their freedom. It's just it's the same old thing. And I know it can be the same old thing within me, too."

"Harry," Asbury said, placing his hand on the driver's arm, "how much of what I've read to you do you remember?"

"About all of it, I'd say, sir," Harry smiled. "I can't read or write a word, but if you read to me, I can remember a story forever. I often wondered why I couldn't read or write, but maybe God let me stay that way 'cos He wanted me to remember His stories better this way." He looked at Asbury, who had a faraway look on his face. "I'm sorry, sir. Is my remembering the Bible a problem?"

"Not a problem, Harry," beamed Asbury, his face set toward the distant tree line. "In fact, you gave me an idea for the future."

"What?" Harry said to the man who had nudged him from behind.

The man, a tall, thin father sitting together with his wife and three girls in their Sunday best, nodded toward the pulpit. "Didn't you hear, brother? Preacher called you up there!" He gestured again toward Asbury, who was waving Harry forward.

In slow, tottering steps, Harry approached the pulpit, remaining on the main floor. "No, Brother Harry!" Asbury insisted, reaching down and pulling Harry upon the platform with him before addressing the congregation. "My driver and brother in Christ, Harry Hosier, cannot preach from the floor. This pulpit belongs to him as well as to me this day!"

Harry could not believe the words coming from Asbury's mouth, but the preacher leaned close and said, "Remember the idea I had when we spoke going north of Greensboro? This is it!"

"What is it?" asked the stunned Harry.

Clapping him on the shoulder, Asbury called out. "Our brother Harry Hosier has a word from the Lord for all of us!"

"A word!" called out one worshiper.

"Preach!" came the voices of others, smiles creasing their faces.

Oh Lord, thought Harry, what do I do now? I've never preached before in my life, let alone to a mixed crowd of black and white. Please Lord, what do I say? I've never felt so empty before.

He stopped. *Empty.* And he knew what to say.

"The message of our Lord Jesus Christ I have for you," Harry thundered, surprising himself and the congregation with his boldness and fervor, "comes from the Gospel of

Luke. It's a parable of our Lord Jesus, it is! He tells us 'A certain man had a fig tree planted in his vineyard; and he came and sought fruit upon it, but found none. Then said he unto the dresser of his vineyard, *Behold, these three years I come seeking fruit on this fig tree, and find none: cut it down; why cumbereth it the ground? And he answering said unto him, Lord, let it alone this year also, till I shall dig about it, and dung it: And if it bear fruit, well: and if not, then after that thou shalt cut it down*.'"[1]

The people were overwhelmed by the fire and passion of Harry's voice. No Bible was before him. He had delivered the Scripture from memory. And then he went on. For over a half-hour he implored the crowd, pleading for their wholehearted devotion, bringing them back constantly to the image of the fig tree. All gathered there, white and black, buzzed with excitement, wept with joy, and nodded their conviction. He closed with a flourish.

"We have before us men and women-folk of separate color today!" Harry gushed. "But we have before us one Word of Almighty God. He comes seeking fruit of goodness, in keeping with His Holy Spirit, on the fig trees of our beings! And He expects fruit from you, and from me! For those of you, born with the same skin as mine: Yes and amen, our Lord calls you to fruitfulness. Remember that He calls you to the fruit of holiness, to bring forth the glorious food of righteousness and the seed of spiritual work in your life. You cannot call Him Savior and then by your waywardness of life ignore His Lordship!"

Harry then looked to the back rows, raising his hands and rubbing his fingers together. "And you who stand here joyful in the Lord's presence and pale as cream in your skin, the Lord calls you to fruitfulness! But that has to do with pruning the bad fruit from the vine of your lives. How the Lord created man—all men, black and white—in

---

1. Luke 13:7-9.

His image, and yet one man enslaves another to upend the Lord's design. No, no! Your spoiled fruit of slavery the Lord Himself desires to prune from our midst, that you might be holy and pleasing in His sight. And He will receive you as you receive your fellow man and woman! This time He warns you, this time He gives you to set it right. The kindness of God is meant to lead all of us to repentance, and the bearing of fruit that our souls be not barren! And if God does this in us, then praise be the name of Jesus!"

The congregation thundered, and rows of people broke out in song and joyous dance. Harry descended from the pulpit to find Asbury and Dr. Rush stepping toward him and pumping his hands.

"Well done, faithful servant," Asbury choked.

"Indeed, Master Harry," Dr. Rush sighed. "The Lord has blessed you to bless us with that, the greatest sermon I have ever heard."

At Adam's Chapel that day, **HARRY HOSIER** became the first Black man to preach to a congregation in America. He followed that in 1784 in Chapeltown, Delaware, by becoming the first Black to preach to an all-white church. Born in Fayetteville, North Carolina, Hosier gained his freedom near the end of the American Revolution and continued to travel with the Methodist bishop Francis Asbury over the growing American frontier, preaching to large gatherings. Although illiterate, Hosier believed God worked through him, gifting him to remember the Bible when read to him so he could faithfully preach. His challenges to personal holiness and the abolition of slavery marked him as a man of conviction who nonetheless exhibited deep humility.

WILLIAM WILBERFORCE

February 23, 1807, House of Commons, London, England

The striking of the gavel barely rose above the rabble of voices within the hall. Members took their time reaching their seats, in stark contrast to the slightly built individual in the front row where members of the Whig Party normally gathered. Those in the know about British politics would have recognized the diminutive man as being fiercely independent in his mind and political character. They also would have known that William Wilberforce's sitting with the Whigs was no surprise. Today was the day this man had waited for, and his labor over the past twenty years was coming to its apex today surrounded by those with whom he had collaborated.

A large, imposing man approached Wilberforce's diminutive form in the front row as more members sat down. Touching Wilberforce on the shoulder, Charles Grey gave the slightest of smiles.

"Dear William," he addressed him, "after many years, today just might be the day you have long desired."

"After that vote in the House of Lords," muttered Wilberforce, his body shaking from anxiety, "I am encouraged. After twenty years of seeking an end to this blasted slave trade, I take nothing for granted."

"And I will be with you today in this attempt" Grey replied excitedly. Looking up at the Speaker's podium, he said, "I'll keep my peace for now. Forgive my excitement, William. I rushed out and drank two cups of tea and am quite full of the stuff ."

"You and your tea, Charles," grinned Wilberforce. "If you're not careful, your name will be synonymous with tea throughout history.[1]"

Charles Abbot[2], the Speaker of the House of Commons, welcomed the members back to the hall before continuing. "The chair recognizes the Honorable Charles Grey."

Patting Wilberforce's knee as he rose, Grey whispered, "The moment is upon us."

The moment is upon us, thought Wilberforce. *How well I remember when that first became true for me.* And he thought back to that wet winter night in Lincolnshire twenty years ago.

For what seemed to be a modest estate to Wilberforce, Langton Hall possessed a spacious dining room that was more than enough room for the eleven people around the table that evening. Wilberforce was amazed to see fellow Parliament members William Windham, Charles Middleton, and Isaac Browne dining with him upon Bennet and Mary Langton's invitation. It appeared to Wilberforce that the dinner had a calculated reason, although he did not let that stop his enjoyment of the meal. The first course of white soup was followed by an excellent beef dish with asparagus and bread. Lord Middleton was especially fond of the vegetables.

"You must thank your cook for her good work, Mrs. Langton," he declared.

"She follows Sarah Phillips[3]," their host replied, "with minimum water and minimum cooking time for vegetables. I'll let her know of your high regard."

---

1. True story: This ended up happening! According to Ione Kramer in the book *All the Tea in China,* Earl Grey tea was named for Charles Grey, although this occurred several years after Grey's death.

2. Charles Abbot (1757-1829) was the Speaker of the House of Commons at this time. The Speaker oversees and maintains debate in the Commons and decides which members will speak on various matters.

3. Sarah Phillips was a cook in English society in the eighteenth century. Her book, *The Ladies' Handmaid,* outlines several techniques that modernized food preparation and cooking in British society.

"Indeed," said Bennet Langton, pressing his napkin into his lap at the head of the table and looking directly at Wilberforce, "but that is not why we are here this evening."

"I had wondered," Wilberforce responded, "given that we have MPs[4] from Norwich, Rochester, and Bridgnorth here." He nodded in turn to Windham, Middleton, and Browne. "Not to mention an eminent young essayist on the subjection of abolition, a member of the Royal Society, a writer, and the premier feminine thinker of our day. Along with Lady Middleton and you, Mr. and Mrs. Langton, this seems to be a groundswell of great importance."

"I will not rebuke you for your insight," said Lord Middleton, "and I thank you for your generosity in your description of our gathering. What we desire is to convince you. Someone must lead Britain out of the darkness of cruelty into the sunlit lands of Christian charity."

Wilberforce glanced at Isaac Browne, who continued.

"I will not say that we are here because of overwhelming reputation," Browne said in his Shropshire accent, sounding like an elegant farmhand. "We are skilled in overseeing labor, or writing as Boswell or young Clarkson here, or growing wealth on our estates. And while four of us stand in Parliament, we know three of us have our limits of influence. That is why you are here, to hear our request to be the influence God has formed you to be."

Wilberforce shifted nervously in his chair. "The abolition of the slave trade? That is what this is all about. Gentlemen, ladies, you know that is an abiding passion of mine. But why do you talk of it as if I should be a leading spokesman?"

"The leading spokesman," said Windham, tossing his napkin on the table for emphasis.

"I am no member of Parliament," Bennet Langton declared, taking a sip of his wine, "but it is clear to us

4. MP is Member of Parliament, one who represents different voting regions in the United Kingdom in the House of Commons.

that you are the key figure who can—no, *must*—lead this charge."

"To abolish slavery?" Wilberforce said, his heart racing. "When so much of the business of the Empire depends on it? My soul is fully against the institution of slavery, but you know what arguments will follow."

"We wish to abolish the African slave trade," Browne said, "which, when it is dried up, would then render the system of slavery throughout the Empire ineffective and useless."

"All of these economic pronouncements are well and good," said Mary Langton, surprising Wilberforce with her vocal force, "but what is at the center of all this is that our African brothers and sisters are made in the image of God! I know that you, Lord Middleton, Mr. Windham, and Mr. Browne have to be patient men, calculating leaders as it were. Legislation is often a river that flows downhill rather than waves that crash upon the beaches of Somerset. But it does not dawdle, Mr. Wilberforce. The question is whether you see the slaves as God's own."

Silence reigned at the table for several moments before Bennet Langton rose from his place at the head of the table.

"Mister Wilberforce...William, if I may," he began. "You have often spoken of being a carriage-wreck of humanity, that you are not worthy to do God's labor. I would ask what other material does a gracious God have to use for His glory?"

Charles Grey's reading of the Abolition of the Slave Trade Bill was eloquent and heartfelt, and the applause thundering in every corner of the House of Commons summoned Wilberforce from his wandering memories. Looking throughout the hall, Wilberforce could see the steely resolve on the faces of a few, those whom he knew to be vehemently opposed to his efforts. He prayed briefly. *Lord Jesus, I have refrained from commenting on this bill for so long, content in Your provision to make a way to free those in need.*

Yet now, I feel compelled to speak one time, to draw everyone within these walls to see Your heart for the slaves and Your Holy Spirit's work within me. Give me Your words, O Lord; give me Your strength.

Raising his hand as the clapping began to subside, Wilberforce waited until Speaker Abbot fully quieted the assembly and called the House to order. Then he continued. "A point of personal privilege to the Honorable William Wilberforce. Master Wilberforce, you have the floor."

The room hushed itself almost immediately, and Wilberforce stood among the members of Parliament in the vast chamber. Looking around, he could scarcely fathom that two decades of hard work, failed votes, more work, near misses, and additional drafting and pleading, had come to this.

"Master Speaker, Master Grey, and all my colleagues within this House who are about to vote on this momentous bill. You may see this as the culmination of several days of debate. I have experienced this as a long journey over the terrain of hope, knowing the promises of Almighty God, and seeking the fulfillment of His goodness, kindness, and abiding hope. This journey has consumed the last twenty years of my life. I say this not to dislodge anyone's conscience, but to demonstrate how intertwined the life of the slaves are with my own."

Taking a deep breath, Wilberforce continued. "I have not shared this with many of you before, though you have heard it in the passage of news and rumor. It may seem strong talk for an Englishman, and to be so outspoken about these convictions risks ridicule in the halls of Westminster.[5] But I am a much different man from the one I used to be. I speak of the urgency of seeing slaves as bearing the image of God. I would ask you also see me in a new light."

5. "Westminster" is a reference to the Palace of Westminster in London. Situated on the north bank of the River Thames, the Palace is the meeting place for both houses of Parliament, the House of Commons and the House of Lords.

Wilberforce went on. "Twenty-three years ago, after I stood for election in Kingston, my mother and sister invited me to come with them on a tour of Europe. As an additional plum, my friend Isaac Milner, the mathematician from Queen's College, was accompanying us. Eventually we found ourselves on the French Riviera. In Nice, Beaulieu-sur-Mer, and Monaco, among other places, and as a young man of twenty-four years of age, all I knew for evening pastimes was a trinity of fine dining, playing cards, and gambling until the early hours of morning, all away from my family and friend Isaac. I returned here to England for a short session of Parliament and then returned to Europe to join Isaac and the family in Genoa. And as surprising as it sounds for a Protestant, I had a spiritual awakening in Italy. When I rejoined them in Genoa, I had endured a difficult journey and I was worried that Pitt's reforms would have some difficulty in our national political climate. I also was pestered by that most vexing of questions. 'Why?' I kept asking myself why I did what I did. Why stand for Parliament? Why give myself over to wine, food, and gambling at such a rough pace? We eventually traveled to Switzerland, and I was walking through Zurich with Isaac one day and I dropped my entire soul at his feet. Everything I did seemed to be so empty. I needed to be assured that what I did mattered, that I wasn't muddling along on Earth passing the days until my breath left my body. Suddenly I burst out, 'I am so empty!', and Isaac, without hesitating, turned to me and said, 'All of which means you need the One who can fill you!'"

Silence reigned in the hall. "If I wished my life to change, I must be changed," Wilberforce went on. "Such a simple turn of phrase! And so we began to pursue that in earnest. The rest of our tour, we read through various books, but what gave me particular delight was the Bible!

That above all else became the air in my lungs and the blood that rushed through my heart! I would rise early every day to read from Scripture, finding peace, finding hope, and above all finding Jesus Christ himself! How crushed I was by my past wanderings and squanderings, believing I was beyond God's mercy. But in Christ, Christ alone, I was offered the grace that cleanses and renews me! Even now I find that overwhelming.

"That is what has compelled me to seek the abolition of the slave trade. Like Abraham of old, I have waited patiently on God to fulfill a hope to which I have been called. This day is a moment when we have to face ourselves and display our deeply held convictions as a nation to the world and to God! Think wisely. Consider carefully. And vote your conscience!"

And with that, William Wilberforce sat down to a shower of applause.

Again the gavel struck several times, bringing the varied conversations through the House of Commons to an end. Charles Abbot rose from his chair to announce the results of the vote, and Wilberforce looked at the floor, balling his hands into fists and slowing his breathing. From his right, Charles Grey placed a kind hand on his shoulder.

"After the vote of the entire House," Abbot's voice rang out like a church bell through the chamber, "I declare the following: Ayes to the right, two hundred and eighty-three votes. Nays to the left, sixteen votes!"

The collective cheers of Wilberforce and Grey's allies split the air, and it was some time before the roars and applause would subside for Abbot's conclusion. "I declare the Act for the Abolition of the Slave Trade through the British Empire ... to be passed!"[6]

6. Although the Act successfully passed in the House of Commons, it still required royal assent by the king. Four weeks later, King George III signed the Act into law.

In that instant, Grey grabbed Wilberforce's hand and pumped it excitedly as dozens of House members swarmed them. The day had finally come, much to Wilberforce's relief and joy, and as more offered him their congratulations, the tears streamed down his cheeks as if they would never end. Eyes closed, he began to softly sing the hymn that rose from his heart.

"Amazing grace! How sweet the sound
that saved a wretch like me!
I once was lost, but now am found,
was blind, but now I see!
'Twas grace that taught my heart to fear,
and grace my fears relieved.
How precious did that grace appear
the hour I first believed!
Through many dangers, toils, and snares
we have already come ...
'Twas grace has brought us safe thus far,
and grace will lead us home!"

The Parliamentary career of **WILLIAM WILBERFORCE** (1759-1833) found him consistently bringing measure after measure to abolish the British slave trade. A firm believer that one's faith led to lively, diligent action for the good of others, Wilberforce was horrified by the treatment of slaves and never gave up hope that the slave trade could be ended. Putting bill after bill before Parliament, Wilberforce endured defeat on these measures, but as more abolitionists were elected in British government, he found increasing support over this twenty-year fight. His pastor, John Newton—himself a former slave ship captain—encouraged his boldness in this effort. Wilberforce himself was able to declare the good news of the bill's passage to Newton, who died soon after this event.

FACT FILES

The Beacons of Freedom and Justice

Freedom is a word that many people value, and we find it mentioned in many contexts. As I write this, Russia and Ukraine are tangled in military conflict, and a word that is often spoken in this context is *freedom*. Film captures this passion, as well. In the movie *Braveheart*, William Wallace cries "Freedom!" before he is executed, and in *Amistad*, the African leader Cinque pleads with the court at the climax of the trial scene by repeating the words, "Give us, us free!"

There is no guarantee of freedom, no matter if we desire it or if it is enshrined in a nation's constitution. Liberty to live in peace and virtue must be sought and preserved. And throughout history, a number of people have desired to give others a place where they could enjoy liberty and tolerance, no matter what their background and no matter what their social standing might be. What can be especially encouraging is when people are motivated by their Christian faith to make that happen. Throughout much of the eighteenth century, we find two men taking such measures.

One such leader who exhibited concern for the freedom of others was **James Oglethorpe** (1696-1785). A decorated soldier in the English Army, Oglethorpe was first elected to Parliament in 1722. His political career was rather undistinguished until one of his good friends died in debtors' prison. These jails had been fashioned as punishment for people who could not pay their debts, and Oglethorpe became concerned for the welfare of the prisoners, reasoning that if they were imprisoned, then how could they be expected to resolve their debts? In addition, Oglethorpe discovered that widespread overcrowding, torture, and disease were rampant in these prisons. Believing the prisoners were worthy of a fresh start, Oglethorpe petitioned for and received a charter to found a new American colony. Selecting an entry point near the Savannah River, the territory would be a buffer between Spanish-held Florida and the British Carolinas. After a voyage of nearly eleven weeks, Oglethorpe and the first group of debtors and other people known as "worthy poor" landed on the shores of what would be the colony of *Georgia*.[1]

The establishment of Georgia was not without trial or difficulty, but Oglethorpe persevered, mainly due to his deep Christian faith. He envisioned Georgia as a community founded on moral and just laws based in biblical religion. Furthermore, he saw the relief granted to debtors and poor people as an example of living out the grace of Jesus Christ in a practical way. Oglethorpe and his investors also showed kindness to the settlers by paying their fares for the voyage and gave them tools for farming and food for meals until they became more self-sufficient. Also, part of Oglethorpe's vision was freedom of worship for Protestant denominations[2] and he maintained good relationships with the Native Americans in the region. In addition, he made known his belief that slavery should be illegal in Georgia, and he sought to keep the rum trade away from the colony's shores. Although future investors changed the complexion and priorities of the colony once Oglethorpe returned to England, his desire to apply his Christian faith to helping those in great need should be applauded.

Another Englishman who promoted freedom was the former slave ship captain **John Newton** (1725-1807). Around eighteen years of age, Newton was forcibly recruited into service with the British Royal Navy, a time

1. Named for King George II, who approved the charter for Oglethorpe.
2. Denominations are groups or subsets of the Protestant faith, such as Anglicans, Presbyterians, Baptists, Methodists, etc.

marked by his attempted desertion for which he was severely punished. He was transferred to the slave ship Pegasus, and when the ship reached Sierra Leone in Africa they left him with a slave dealer named Amos Clowe. He forced Newton into slavery to his wife, who had Newton treated savagely. Thankfully, in 1748, he was rescued and returned to England aboard a ship called Greyhound. Not only had this voyage been arranged at the request of Newton's father, it turned out to be a significant moment for Newton's life. The ship was battered by a storm off Ireland's coast and all seemed lost; Newton prayed earnestly for God's protection, and the storm died away. This was a moment that cause Newton to look more deeply at Scripture and other books about Christianity. Although he captained ships in the slave trade for another six years, Newton viewed slaves through sympathetic and kinder eyes. In 1754, he ended his ship captaining career.

While Newton continued to financially invest in the slave trade, a gradual spiritual metamorphosis continued inside of him. He began to speak out in favor of the abolition of slavery throughout the British Empire. Eventually, Newton trained for the ministry in the Church of England, learning theology and the biblical languages of Hebrew and Greek while he served as a collector of revenue in Liverpool. While this took considerable time and effort, eventually Newton was ordained an Anglican priest in Olney and in 1779 was invited to serve as rector of St. Mary Woolnoth Church in London. This location gave him considerable access to a growing number of younger churchgoers and government officials. His friendship and influence with William Wilberforce (who is mentioned elsewhere in this book) convinced the young Wilberforce to remain in Parliament and take up the causes of freedom and justice. This led to a determined and lengthy attempt to abolish the British slave trade, a key element in the eventual toppling of the institution of slavery. Newton rejoiced to see the slave trade abolished during his lifetime prior to his death in 1807.

Through his fight for freedom and justice, Newton never lost sight that he was an undeserving recipient of God's grace which had freed him from his sin and rebellion. He expressed his gratitude to the Lord through his many hymns which are still sung in churches today, among them "Amazing Grace", "How Sweet the Name of Jesus Sounds", and "Glorious Things of Thee Are Spoken".

While men like Oglethorpe and Newton came from England and used the extension of freedom as an example of Christian mercy, the institution of slavery was still an ugly eyesore on the landscape of America. Over time, a group of people known as abolitionists sought to educate people and confront owners about the evils of the chattel slavery[3] of Blacks. As long as Blacks did not have freedom to live as they could in America, they declared, they did not have true justice, for they did not have the access they deserved in order to improve their lives. Both Whites and Blacks were involved in this process, but two individuals who merit particular consideration for their actions were former slaves themselves.

Speaker, writer, and preacher **Frederick Douglass** (1817-1895) became one of the most forceful leaders in the abolition movement. Born in slavery on Maryland's eastern shore, Douglass was separated from his mother when an infant and lived with his grandparents, who were slaves. Eventually, when he was almost ten, Douglass was sent to serve the Auld family in Baltimore.

3. Chattel slavery—as opposed to indentured servitude or slaves captured in war—occurs when people are considered the legal property of an owning class, and they can be bought, sold, and kept forever in the condition of slavery.

Douglass later described the wife, Sophia Auld, as a kind woman who treated him as one should treat a human being. He learned the alphabet from her, which led to his gaining an ability to read and he kept teaching himself in subsequent years.

Believing that knowledge was the pathway to freedom, the more Douglass read, the more he was convinced of the repulsiveness of slavery. Although he endured more years of back-breaking cruelty at the hands of other slave-owners, Douglass eventually boarded a train in Baltimore dressed as a sailor and carrying identification papers he received from a free Black sailor. He traveled into Delaware and then took a steamboat across the river to Philadelphia, Pennsylvania and freedom, continuing onward to New York City over a harrowing twenty-four-hour escape. Eventually settling in Massachusetts with his new bride, Douglass joined the African Methodist Episcopal Zion church and became a licensed preacher in 1839. His skills of communication displayed power and passion, and he soon used his biblical convictions to join the abolition movement and speak against the evils of slavery, publishing an abolitionist newspaper called the *North Star.* He believed that education was essential for Blacks to improve their lives and break the yoke of slavery, even more important than gaining the right to vote. He spoke out against the hypocrisy of American ministers who supported slavery. He believed in the urgency of other Blacks playing their part in speaking out against slavery. He also believed in persuasion and dialogue with slave owners and people of differing perspectives. Changing hearts, he acknowledged, was critical as part of changing laws. In response to criticism of this broad approach, Douglass declared to an audience in Rochester, New York, "I would unite with anybody to do right and with nobody to do wrong."

In addition to Douglass' passionate and patient approach, the former slave **Harriet Tubman** (1822-1913) risked her personal safety to ensure that other slaves could escape from their owners and find freedom elsewhere. Like Frederick Douglass, she grew up in slavery on the Eastern Shore of Maryland. There, she loved the Bible stories her mother told her, and she found great inspiration in the book of Exodus where Moses led the Hebrews out of slavery in Egypt. Also like Douglass, she escaped, ending up in Philadelphia. Rather than merely speaking out against slavery, Tubman viewed herself as a "stranger in a strange land" and sought to bring freedom to those under slavery's power. Guided by her Methodist faith and her unwavering conviction that if she was free, then others should be free, Tubman would return to slave states time and again and guide slaves along escape routes northward. When the Congress of the United States passed the Fugitive Slave Law in 1850, it made her work more difficult. The law punished anyone assisting the escape of slaves and forced officials to help capture runaway slaves, even in states where slavery was illegal. In spite of the risks, Tubman tirelessly worked to bring slaves to freedom in expeditions known as the "Underground Railroad", bringing them to northern cities where they could find work and also to Canada. She often worked during winter when the nights were longer and people stayed in their homes, reducing the likelihood she would be discovered in action. She would wear many disguises and often pretend she was running errands. Since her enemies knew she was illiterate, Tubman would sometimes take newspapers or books and pretend to read to throw them off the chase. Due to her bravery and success, she was called "Moses", and she never failed in any mission or lost anyone on the "Underground Railroad". She always trusted God would protect her, and whenever she would successfully transfer the newly freed slaves, she would exclaim, "Glory to God and Jesus, too! Another is safe!" Her deep faith always inspired her to provide freedom from earthly slavery as Christ gives freedom from spiritual slavery.

Providing freedom and justice often means stepping out in faith and taking risks. But part of being a follower of Jesus is letting go of what is safe in order to be faithful. Such is the legacy of those who fought for others who couldn't fight for themselves.

EMILIE MALLET

June 1832, Paris, France

The shrieks could be heard flying through the air in every direction. As normally hardy men, durable women, and their poor children wailed from their homes in the slums, these screams were of an entirely different order, thought Emilie. The squalor of the city streets, the poor drainage, and the fetid odor of the unwashed crowds created a stench that she had not experienced in her lifetime. But these scratchy roars from human throats were not originating from the slums, but from the roads to the southwest. Turning to her driver, Emilie covered her mouth with a cloth and gasped, "The cries are particularly sharp in that direction."

"They are, m'lady," said Laurent, who had served her well for ten years, "and they seem to be coming from near the Pantheon, which makes sense given the news I've heard."

"What news?" Emilie asked.

Laurent covered his mouth with a kerchief of his own. "The mob is angry, m'lady. You heard of the death of the Prime Minister, of course?"

"I did, but what do these spasms of fear have to do with that?"

"The cholera that is consuming the city took Monsieur Perier," Laurent replied, "and that was satisfaction enough for many in the slums, at least those in the silk factories. He'd been the one that crushed their workers' strike last year with guns and clubs. But the king insisted on giving him a state funeral at the Pantheon."

"Hence the rage throughout the *arrondissiment*[1]," Emilie mumbled. "So they are storming the Pantheon as if it was the Bastille? But why? His death was four weeks ago."

Laurent grabbed her by the arm and pulled her out of the way of a wailing pack of children who ran by, shaking their fists in the direction of the mob. "Begging your pardon, m'lady, but we need to get you to safety. Across the bridge to the Cathedral[2] and we can find our wagon there."

As Laurent helped her into the carriage, Emilie said, "Monsieur Mallet will be only too relieved if we make it back unscathed, but before we leave this place, you will tell me what else you know."

"What do you mean, m'lady?" Laurent blanched.

"Because it's written on your face. And because you have worked for me for a decade," Emilie sternly replied. "The mob's roars have changed. Why?"

Laurent swallowed hard. "This is just based on rumors I heard. The crowd is upset that the king gives Perier a state funeral, but refused one to General Lemarque who also died of cholera just two days ago."

"He was a war hero!" exclaimed Emilie. "Why would the king ever do something so graceless and heavy-handed?"

"That's what I need to tell you," Laurent urged her. "I overheard two servants discussing it while you were dining with Madam Fignon. A massive swell of people intends to take the general's coffin and forcibly march on the Pantheon to give him a proper burial to defy the king."

The horrible realization of what this meant suddenly

---

1. An *arrondissiment* is an administrative district of larger French cities, like Paris.
2. That would be Notre Dame Cathedral. Construction of the cathedral began in 1163 and was largely finished by 1260.

dawned on Emilie Mallet. "So, those screams are not of agony or fear from suffering families." She wiped aside a tear of heartbrokenness. "This is rage. This is an uprising."

"All of which requires me to insist we leave now, m'lady," Laurent said, practically pushing her hand off the frame of the carriage door and shutting her in. "If we are to get you home, we can't wait. Jouy-en-Josas is well over an hour's drive from here in perfect conditions."

"Wait!" Emilie called. Laurent had one foot on the step to the calash[3] , but he obediently halted.

Emilie peeked her head out the carriage window. "I am sorry, Laurent, but if we are to return home, I wish to do so with a clear conscience. We are facing a city in the throes of death. We are leaving a city about to be torn by rebellion. We have heard the chief of police slander the poor by saying they have deliberately poisoned the Seine[4] and turned a mist of cholera loose throughout Paris to bring down the aristocracy. I fully recognize your desire to get to safety. But there are many here in the city who cannot fend for themselves."

"Then what does m'lady command?" asked Laurent, already dreading the answer.

Pointing back across the bridge spanning the Seine, Emilie ordered, "Into the slums. Now."

"Why?" Laurent demanded.

"Because as our Savior once went into the most vile places to seek the lost," Emilie shot back, "so will we!"

The first stop they made was by a rusted water pump on the Rue Adolphe Adam. Laurent pulled the horses to a stop where filthy puddles blotched the ground. Here

---

3. A calash (or French caliche) is a wheeled vehicle driven by horses, with seats for two to four people, and a splashboard up front where the driver or coachman would sit.
4. The Seine is the main river that runs through Paris.

the wails from the home grew particularly desperate, even drowning out the cries from the Pantheon in the distance. Alighting from the carriage herself, Emilie walked up to the door of the first house she saw. Knocking firmly upon it, she was shocked that the barest force sent the door collapsing inward off its rusty hinges. Laurent, standing behind her, shook his head. "About the same condition as the Cathedral," he scoffed. Ignoring him, Emilie walked in, covering her mouth.

"Hello!" she called into the darkness. "Hello! Is anyone here?"

A cough and groan sounded from the back room, and the tattered folds of a curtain that hung in the rear doorway gently moved aside as a little girl eased herself through the frame. Her dirty dress hung from her body, which was horribly thin. Her face, though pretty, was bony and smudged with grime, and when she spoke, both Emilie and Laurent could see some of her teeth were missing and those that remained were poorly colored. Emilie slowly approached her and even at her deliberate pace, the girl hung back, quivering like a frightened rabbit.

"You are safe, little mademoiselle," Emilie softly spoke. "I have not come here to harm you. I take it you are afraid to go out?"

The little girl nodded vigorously, tears glistening in her eyes. "I hear the cries," she sobbed, "and there is much anger about. Some of the people stopped here to enlist our family in the march on the Pantheon, but mother turned them out. And one burly fellow looked at me angrily and said, 'Then I'll be back for you later!' That was an hour ago."

"Is it you and your mother who live here?" Emilie said, stooping down to be at eye level with the girl.

"Our whole family," the girl shuddered. "My brother Jean and my parents..." She never got to complete the sentence as a woman stumbled from the back room, her apron streaked with an unpleasant color and emitting an even more unpleasant odor.

"Are you them threateners come back?" she asked.

Emilie shook off Laurent's hand attempting to pull her away. "We are not, madam. I am Emilie Mallet. Your daughter was explaining to me that she and your son might be in danger if the crowd returns."

"A plague on them worse than the one we have now!" spat the mother. "I am here trying to care for my husband before he dies of the cholera, and I have to worry about my Julie and Jean!" She began to cry.

And in that moment, Emilie knew exactly what to do.

"This is madness, m'lady," Laurent called over his shoulder as he madly drove the carriage, sending it careening through the streets of Paris as they headed west for Versailles, where they could then turn southward toward home. Eight little children were squeezed into the carriage with Emilie, their eyes wide as tea-saucers and their teeth chattering with fear. Only Julie spoke up. "Ma'am, what do you mean by taking us from Paris? What did you tell our parents?"

Emilie reached over and patted Julie's hand. "There, there, sweet Julie, it's natural you wish to ask. With the cholera in Paris, and with the threats of the crowd, we need to find you dear children somewhere safe."

"How will we know when we can go back?" asked another child, a boy.

"Completely natural to ask that, as well, young man," Emilie replied. "I asked your parents' permission to take you to a safe place, noted your dwellings, and so we can return you in due course. But the center of Paris is no place for children. I am taking you to my house in Jouy-en-Josas."

"Is that even in France?" teased Jean. The children, for the first time, laughed uproariously.

"Indeed it is," Emilie replied, chuckling herself. "It is where my brother had his factory and where I live with my husband."

"I wish I hadn't had to leave behind some of my friends," said another girl.

Emilie paused, then called up to Laurent. "Laurent! Alert the horsemen at the house to hitch other carriages! I will need them and you to make several journeys before nightfall!" As they drove on, she closed her eyes and prayed. *Lord Jesus, I do not know what will become of this endeavor. But give me the strength to love these children well as I become a part of their lives.*

The carriages had set off for Paris again, and Emilie had managed to locate bedrooms in the great house. Upon their arriving, the children had gasped their collective amazement, which caused Emilie to realize none of them had been in a house of this size before, let alone one with shiny windows, and a properly gabled roof.

Many of the children were being attended to in the smaller dining room, and Emilie was content to allow the kitchen staff to sort out an evening meal for them. Retreating to the library, she sat down wearily upon a couch. Letting out a groan, Emilie again bowed her head. Several minutes went by while she simply opened her heart to receive the peace and reassurance that only the Holy Spirit could bring. Emilie did not know how she would care for all these children but she trusted that the Lord would guide her. *It is a time,* she told herself, *to step forward in faith, and God will show the path to take.*

She felt the presence of someone before her, and when Emilie opened her eyes, she saw Julie standing there. Dressed in a white blouse and red skirt, the little girl stood before Emilie, her face washed and looking much fairer than when Emilie first saw her in the Paris slums.

"Welcome to my home, Julie," she said.

"Thank you, madam," Julie replied, looking around the room. Emilie realized that the child had never seen a book before, let alone a whole library. Allowing her eyes to rest on two books on a nearby table, Julie pointed to them and asked, "What are those?"

Emilie picked up the first volume and patted the cover. "These are books that are part of this library, this room. My husband and I have collected them over the years."

Julie looked downward, somewhat embarrassed. "I cannot read, ma'am," she said softly.

"There is no shame in that, darling, given the hard life you've been given thus far," Emilie said, patting Julie's face, "but if you like, while you're here, I can teach you how to read."

Picking up one of the volumes on the table Emilie smiled, "This one is a new book, printed just last year. A writer named Victor Hugo. I've only read some of it, but it's a tale that seems worth reading. A story set at Notre Dame in the city."

Julie looked thoughtful, then pointed at the other one. "And that?"

Emilie took her well-worn Bible in her hands. "This, dear Julie, is the most wonderful story imaginable. A story of love. A story of a man who came to rescue the people he loved. This is the story of Jesus Christ."

"Of Jesus?" Julie said, her eyes dropping. "I know a little about him. Sometimes my father says his name, rather loudly, when he drops things. I also hear the priests in Paris pray to him, but those priests put my uncle in debtors' prison, so I'm not partial to them."

Emilie drew close and placed her arm around Julie. "My dear, I am so sorry that your uncle was treated so by those who speak the name of Jesus. Given time, perhaps we can change what they have done. But I can give you safety here, and, I will read to you about how Jesus gave me safety."

Julie looked up at her, eyes shining. "How did he do that?"

"He rescued me," Emilie said, softly. "Oh, not from debtor's prison, or from a house in the dirt and grime of Paris, or from an invading army. No, Jesus rescued me from my sin, from my hatred of what is good. And he did that by dying for me, and because of his death, he changed my heart."

For the first time in ever such a long time, Julie smiled. "Why did Jesus do that, ma'am?"

"Indeed, I ask myself that every day, sweet one," Emilie replied, "and all I can say is that he loved me. Not because I was good, but despite who I am. Jesus loves me simply because he wants to love me."

In an age of unrest and disease, **EMILIE MALLET** became a dedicated Protestant Christian woman seeing to the needs of poor children and prisoners in the Paris area. The daughter of Christophe Oberkampf, who produced the famous Toile de Jouy printed cotton fabric, Emilie married into a banking family and was used to an upper-class life. Yet her Christian faith drove her to minister to those in dire circumstances. In both cholera epidemics (1832 and 1849), she sheltered children from Paris' slums away from the disease's ravages. Her "shelters" became nursery schools for children from working-class families. She also led efforts to visit prisoners and care for those recently released from jail, helping them rejoin French society. Her desire for her faith to bear fruitful action inspired other prominent women to join her in fighting many of the social issues of the day, seeking to be Christ's servant to those on the margins of society.

CHARLES SPURGEON

August-September 1854, Southwark, London

The stairs leading to the pulpit in the Baptist church creaked under his steps, but Charles Spurgeon had every confidence they would bear him up. He laid his Bible upon the wooden lectern and peered over it, casting a kindly gaze to the gathered congregation. Truly God had been merciful to him in granting him a flock so hungry for the preaching of the Word. How many pastors three times his age would give anything for such an assembly at any point in their ministries. Yet the Lord, in His grace, had seen fit to give him such fine folk week after week when he was at the age of twenty! Indeed, the New Park Street Chapel had taken a chance on him, both due to his youth and since he trusted in Christ just five years prior. *All I pray,* Spurgeon thought as he readied himself to preach, *is that I reward their trust and that you, Lord, speak through me. Amen.*

Taking a deep breath, Spurgeon began. "I take as my text today First Samuel chapter twelve and the seventeenth verse in which the prophet Samuel reminds Israel, 'Is it not wheat harvest today?' To us gathered here in Park Street today, I shall simply take these words as a motto; and my sermon will be founded upon a harvest field. I suppose the dwellers in cities think less of times and seasons than dwellers in the country. Men who were born, trained up, nourished and nurtured among corn-fields, harvests, sowings, and reapings, are more likely to notice such things than you who are always engaged in mercantile pursuits, and think less of these things than rustics do. But I suppose, if it is almost necessary that you should less regard the harvest than others, it ought not to be carried to too great an extent. Let us not be forgetful of times and seasons. There is much to be learned from them, and I would refresh your memories by a harvest field."[1]

Many of the people nodded their assent, and for the next forty minutes Spurgeon winsomely developed his theme of God's harvest, speaking plainly and directly. He drew out biblical reminders of three joyful harvests, the harvests of fields, of the life of the Christian, and of the work of Jesus Christ Himself. He followed that with reminders of sad harvests, of death, of wickedness, and of the wrath of God against evil. His speaking was simple, mostly with one-syllable words in a pace that refused to drag. The dwellers of Southwark were a wide range of educations, but the less learned appreciated his simplicity, and even the more sophisticated found his messages to be quite meaty.

He slowed his speech and plunged into the difficult words about death: "Oh, that great reaper; he sweeps through the earth, and mows his hundreds and thousands down! It is all skill; death makes no noise about his movements, and he treads with velvet footfall over the earth; that ceaseless mower, none can resist him. He is irresistible, and he mows, and mows, and cuts them down. Sometimes he stops and whets his scythe[2]; he dips his scythe in blood, and then he mows us down with war; then he takes his whetstone[3] of cholera, and mows down more than ever."

It was the mention of cholera when Spurgeon felt the pang in his heart. It wasn't a physical pain so much as a darkness, a foreboding, a premonition of something sinister. *Why did I sense that?* He wondered. *We have had*

1. Many thanks to Midwestern Baptist Theological Seminary's Spurgeon Center for Biblical Preaching, which had this sermon (which I have condensed and modified for readability) online at https://www.spurgeon.org/resource-library/sermons/harvest-time/#flipbook/

2. A scythe is a curved blade used for harvesting grain.

3. A whetstone is a stone block used for sharpening knives or other tools.

outbreaks here in London before and have soldiered on. So why did I have a sudden sensation of dread at that word?

Putting the thought aside, he went on, finally closing his sermon with a flourish. "You shall have a harvest in due season if you faint not. Sow on, brother; sow on, sister; and in due time thou shalt reap an abundant harvest. Go on, and in due season, by God's mighty grace, you shall reap if you do not give up."

The closing hymn, his benediction, and even the line of people to shake his hand after the service were a blur to Spurgeon. Looking back, he would weep at the realization that some of these people packed into the chapel that day would not live to see Christmas.

He woke with a start in the darkness. Always in the darkness. Spurgeon tore the bedclothes from atop him and wiped the sweat from his forehead. He was still not sleeping through the night, having nightmares of one funeral service after another. Stumbling to his wash-basin, he cupped his hands in the lukewarm water and splashed it over his face, repeating the action twice more as if continued washings could cleanse the filth and illness he sensed all around him. He checked his face in the looking glass and saw his skin more drawn and sallow. His eyes bore the beginnings of darkened circles beneath them. Rest had become a luxury he could not afford, and now he had more pastoral calls to make, more ill church members to visit, more prayers to lift to God on their behalf when he was unsure if his cries were getting through to heaven.

Spurgeon left his house and, after a few turns, made his way to the Great Dover Road and headed southeast in Southwark. How quickly this borough had changed after the outbreak of cholera in Westminster just across the river. The fingers of death had reached out from Broad and Cambridge Street, and now clutched at any resistance within Southwark and the nearby areas. Few shops were open; those that braved the epidemic had signs posted warning any who showed signs of cholera to stay away. All things had caused an even more sad reality to infect Southwark, Spurgeon thought. It was the grip of fear that gave others so much dread.

Two blocks from the Sidney residence and his visit with their dangerously ill grandfather, Spurgeon caught a pebble in his shoe. Stopping, he took off his bowler hat, waggled the stone from his shoe, and straightened himself up. Looking at himself in a butcher's window, he burst into tears. *I am only twenty years old, and I look a hundred! How am I to be a faithful pastor and preacher if I wear myself out now?*

He reached the Sidney house when he realized he hadn't wiped the tears away.

"I beg your pardon being late with the tea," Jenny Sidney apologized breathlessly. "It just so happens to be Pa's favorite time of the day. Will you be wanting tea, Reverend? It's hot and strong."

"I will, if your Pa is having some," Spurgeon answered hoarsely. Jenny then brought a tray on which two cups and a teapot were placed over a plain cloth. She insisted on pouring the tea and then propped her father-in-law up in his bed so he could drink properly.

"He doesn't have much strength to speak," Jenny explained as she fluffed the pillows, "and I may have to excuse you if we have to change the sheets suddenly, and please be aware if he is suddenly sick everywhere. However, he likes having you here."

"I am not certain how much of a strength I can be for him," Spurgeon said, sipping his drink. "I have seen enough of sickness and death these past weeks to know that I am helpless against them. Oh Pa Sidney," he said, looking at the aged man writhing in the bed, "how I wish I could remove your pain. I know only God can do so, and yet this disease marches on and on. I can only pray with and for you, and also commend you to Christ who can deliver you." He stopped, his own mind seeking powerful words of comfort, but he could not bring them forth. "I am sorry," he continued, "that I am such a poor help in this time."

Pa garbled something. Spurgeon leaned closer but couldn't make out his words. Jenny smiled and helped translate her father-in-law's mumbled words.

"Reverend Spurgeon," she lilted softly. "He means to say that he appreciates your company. Don't worry if you feel you have nothing to say. Your presence is enough. He believes it's like the angel who strengthened Jesus in the garden when our Lord was anguished. Just being at his bedside is enough."

Spurgeon fought back his surging emotions. "Those are such kind words, Jenny," he replied, "and yet I don't believe I deserve them. I thought at my age I'd be full of strength, but I have come to realize my limitations. I preach my sermons, but they seem so removed from this present battle for so many."

"Oh, don't say that, Charles!" Jenny exclaimed, surprising Spurgeon with her use of his first name. "Remember what you preached last month about the harvests. You even mentioned the cholera in passing. I'd say that showed great foresight. Just because we suffer now, that doesn't mean we won't reap the good harvest that God can give us."

"I would hope for that, Jenny," Spurgeon sighed, noting that Pa had fallen into a gentle sleep. "At first I threw myself into my visits with my vigor. I thought, I am twenty, I have the inner strength. But I have lost count of the bedsides at which I have sat. Almost daily I stand by the grave of someone I knew. Their bodies give out and their hearts expire, and I am weary in body and sick at heart. I practically have no reserves left, and I wonder if my grave will be dug in a matter of weeks.

I'm sorry! That was intemperate and showed no trust in the God I proclaim!" He put his head in his hands.

"Reverend," Jenny said gently without a trace of impatience, "anyone could forgive you for experiencing such worries. And I don't have the answer for you on my lips, but remember what you preached to us last month."

Spurgeon looked up. "And what was that?"

Jenny straightened in her chair. "You said, 'Go on, and in due season, by God's mighty grace, you shall reap if you do not give up.' I'd say that's a message you could use now."

"Indeed, I could," he said, "although I'd need reminded of it constantly in order to not give up."

Jenny reached across to take his tea cup. "Perhaps you'll find that good word in the most unlikely of places."

Jenny's encouragement seemed to be miles away the next day as Spurgeon walked slowly down the Great Dover Road, after yet another funeral. The gray clouds made the London day even more dreary. He was within sight of the Sidney residence again, but he couldn't bring himself to go in for fear that Pa would die in front of him. A cascade of weariness and helplessness crashed through him. Leaning over, he put his hands on his knees and uttered a prayer.

"Lord, I am so overwhelmed. I have nothing left. What am I to do?"

And in that moment the words of Jenny Sidney came to mind. *Perhaps you'll find that good word in the most unlikely of places.*

He straightened up and turned to his right. There before him was a cobbler's shop. The window had chips of old paint flecked on its edges but was otherwise surprisingly clean. However, the window pane wasn't what arrested Spurgeon's sight. It was a large sheet of paper posted on it. Taking a step closer, Spurgeon stood, mouth open, as he read the words printed on it in large, bold handwriting:

"Because thou hast made the Lord, which is my refuge, even the Most High, thy habitation, there shall no evil befall thee, neither shall any plague come nigh thy dwelling." [4]

Nothing else seemed to move around him; to Spurgeon, it felt like time stood still. And yet, he felt in an instant as if the weight of the world had fallen from his shoulders. The promise of God from that psalm immediately pierced his heart like an arrow full of joy and peace!

"Lord God," he said aloud, oblivious to whomever heard him and walking with a new spring in his step, "thank you for your Word given to me. Maintain this calm and peaceful spirit within me as I visit the sick and dying. As these words have caused me to feel secure and refreshed in your power, continue to uphold me! Give strength to me as I serve you, as I preach your Word, as I shepherd your people. O Lord, you are eternally good! May your Spirit work through me all the days of my life!"

It was no coincidence, he thought as his stroll picked up pace, that the clouds parted at that moment, and the sun gloriously beamed down upon him.

For nearly thirty-eight years, **CHARLES SPURGEON** served as the pastor of the New Park Street Chapel, which changed its name to the Metropolitan Tabernacle. A faithful and diligent preacher, he spoke several times a week at the church, which could hold over five thousand people for services. Speaking plainly and enthusiastically about Jesus Christ, he preached nearly 3,600 sermons and wrote almost fifty books. A conscientious and loving pastor, Spurgeon also visited churchgoers and established schools, founded an orphanage, and formed groups to help the poor and marginalized. He also founded a pastor's college in London to train future church leaders. In all, Spurgeon never forgot his continuous need for the grace of God shown through Jesus Christ, and he delighted to sharing this good news with others.

4. Psalm 91:9-10.

SOJOURNER TRUTH

May 29, 1851, Akron, Ohio

The crowd outside the church grew louder and more heated in their declarations, making the warm Ohio air seem a few degrees higher. Thousands milled about, their passions rising as they waited on the next speaker. Sojourner Truth, her graying hair worn in a plait behind her head, approached the stage from the side. Making her way through the mass of females young and old, her hands, toughened by her years of spinning wool on the estates in New York, she slid amongst the bodies before her, trying to part them like Moses divided the Red Sea with God's almighty help.

Sojourner sensed their emotions. At best, many of these women were indifferent to her presence. At worst, they were downright hostile. And it wasn't just the women, most of the men of this area were absolutely indignant to a days-long meeting about women's liberties . The resistance was so stiff she felt as if she was pushing against the brick houses of her masters from years ago.

She slipped as she reached the church steps, knocking herself sideways into a young woman wearing a bright green hat and possessing equally piercing green eyes. The young lady's burning glare could have started a forest fire.

"Where do you think you're going, ma'am?" the girl sneered. "Aren't you to be at the back?" She pointed to the rear of the crowd.

"Nothing new in what you're saying, miss," Sojourner retorted, drawing her petite self to as full a height as she could muster, "though sad to hear it all the same. It just so happens I'm speaking to this crowd of which you are a part."

"I don't believe a word you're saying, madam," came the shrill reply of another woman, tall and thin as a rail. "It's bad enough we have a deluge of the local clergy out to denounce our meeting, but you are certainly not helping."

"You don't even know who I am, by sight or name," replied Sojourner as she waved her darkened hands before her and then pointed back at herself for emphasis. "All you see is the color of my skin and off you go pronouncing judgment worse than the men carping at all of us."

"The fact we don't know who you are is one such problem," quipped the first woman.

"It's not that you look at me and see me looking like a charcoal bit in a bowl of milk and you squirm away?" Sojourner replied hotly. "Then I'll give proof!" She pointed to the stage in front of the Old Stone Church. "Missus Gage! Have you room up there as promised?"

A curly-haired female, clad in a dark blue dress, turned her head and, above the tumult of the crowd, saw her petitioner. "Mrs. Truth! Mrs. Truth! As promised, indeed! I have room here for you!"

"You know Frances Gage?" said the incredulous women in unison.

"Missus Gage knows me," replied Sojourner Truth in a gracious but firm tone. "Now, if you'll excuse me." And she moved past them to ascend the stage.

Frances Gage brooked no protests. One look from her would freeze the haughtiest protestor, although there were still men standing well away from the expansive crowd who snipped and chortled at whomever spoke from the makeshift stage. Punctuating the air with her index finger, Gage reminded the gathered assembly they were there for a unified purpose before introducing the woman next to her.

"We have gathered to address the rights of women everywhere, but this nation must see the clear link between those rights and the freedom of the Black race. To pretend that the smile of God passes over and ignores our Black sisters and brothers is to ignore the way that God has created us, His very children! And so today, I call each of you to come with clean hearts and curious minds to hear the words of this woman, one without peer in her difficulties, her desire for freedom, and her willingness to see the hope and justice of God meld together on behalf of women everywhere! I give you, my sisters of the present struggle, Sojourner Truth!"

The jeers had disappeared, but the applause was not overwhelming. *No matter,* thought Sojourner. *The Lord is my audience, and He shall receive the glory this day. Lord Jesus, be my strength!* She looked out at the crowd of women. *No matter their initial coldness,* she told herself, they were her sisters this day. She would win them over. Oh, with the help of Jesus, she would win them over!

"My sisters of the struggle, of many struggles become one, I greet you this day in the power of God!" she began. "Had you known me but a decade ago, you would know me as Isabella Baumfree, daughter of James and Elizabeth, slaves in New York state! You would have been surprised at the crisp elocution of this girl who knew Dutch as her first language. You would have seen before you a woman once sold for one hundred dollars to the harshest of men in Kingston. And even that is not the whole story, for I was sold away from my dear parents that day with a flock of sheep thrown into the bargain. Me and the lambs for money! And sold again, and sold again. In the clutches of a man who beat me with rods. Even today, O sisters, my back tells the story of hundreds of beatings, and those were not even the most unspeakable, the darkest things my master did to me!"

Sojourner swayed, tears coming to her eyes as she relived the memories and the horror. "Spinning wool was my craft of force, even after my master promised to free me and went back on his word. A man holding power over a woman, white holding power over black. This is my story, and it only grows and grows. Where I go, it follows as I follow my Lord Jesus! They took my son from me, daring me to take him back as was my right! And I took my former master to court, and I—a Black woman who sued a white master—I won. Never before in this land had anyone seen the like, but my Lord works miracles, because He is the God of the impossible!"

The crowd's murmurs, barely audible at first, had swelled into a rumble. Even some "amens" began to be heard from the rear of the assembly. "And this God and King uses me to proclaim to you today that the impossible ends here! It ends in Akron! It ends in America! He uses me as He first called me eight years ago on that holy day known as Pentecost. It was in that blessed Methodist chapel that the Spirit of the Lord drew me forth. It was then that I heard that still, small voice, sure as Elijah the prophet did on Mount Sinai many years ago. Proclaim the truth, my God moved me! Proclaim the truth for as long as you will sojourn on the earth, was His word to me. I told my friends that day, 'The Holy Spirit calls me, and I must go. I must sojourn on and proclaim His truth, and hence, I changed my name to that what you have heard Missus Gage say already!"

"I go on to say," she continued, waving her hands like a Midwestern wheat field in a prairie breeze as the women began to clap and chant her name, "that what Almighty God has made clear through His Word and His Spirit, I tell you today: The subjugation of any man or woman to slavery on account of the color of skin, whether in the cotton fields of the South or the wool looms of the North, is as poison in the mouth of our Savior God!" The word *poison* lit a fire within the hearts of her hearers, and roars peppered the crowd even as the searing heat of the late May sun beat down upon their heads. "And the freedom that is pressed upon us by virtue of being in the image of God leads to more. I have proclaimed the truth of abolition of the yoke of slavery. Now I pray we take on another yoke."

Palms down, she signaled for quiet, even though absolute silence was out of the question. Nor did the remaining noise bother her. Indeed, it only served to stoke her intensity even more. "We come to the steps of God's church today as among those who are treasured by the Lord God Himself. Remember that Adam did all that he was commanded in Eden, naming every beast of God's creation, and yet as the Word of God has said, for Adam there was not a helper fit for him. And we have those precious and resounding words from the mouth of the Lord Himself: 'It is *not good* that the man should be alone!'

"My fellow women, my fellow helpers, of whom God Himself has declared that our absence would be a detriment to the goodness of His world: I tell you this day that breaking our yoke of no suffrage, of eliminating the gulf between us and men and giving us equal rights, is the goal set before us!"

The women raised their voices in a unified chorus, urging Truth on. She did not disappoint.

"I must say," Truth continued, "if there is noise about this matter, then there must be something worth repairing. We have the Black women of the South and the women here in the North all talking about their God-given rights, everyone will want to know what the matter is. I'll tell you straightaway what it is." She pointed at the clergymen across the street that guffawed at her every sentence. "You men, I tell you now: I personify a woman's rights! I have as much muscle as any man, and can do as much work as any man. I have plowed and reaped and husked and chopped and mowed, and can any man do more than that? You show me your labor? I ask you to come beside me and see my arms, and feel the sinews within them! I have heard much about the sexes being equal, and that's more than just words. I can carry as much as any man, and can eat as much too, if I can get it. I am as strong as any man that is now!"

Now all the ladies were yelling for more, their voices like a storm on the Great Lakes, and Truth continued. "As for intellect, all I can say is, if a woman have a pint, and a man a quart — why can't she have her little pint full? You men don't need to be afraid to give us our rights for fear we will take too much. We can't take more than our pints will hold. Why men, if you can give a woman rights, give it to her and you will feel better. You will have your own rights, and they won't be so much trouble.

Pacing the stage, Truth balled her hands into fists, feeling the sweat ooze from her palms. Never before had she felt as joyous as she did at that moment. "Listen to me! I can't read...not a word. But most certainly, I can hear a word and not forget it. I have heard the Bible and I have learned that Eve caused man to sin. Well, if a woman upset the world, do give us women a chance to set it right side up again. Remember if you will the Lord Jesus! He never spurned women at any time. Recall the words of the apostle when Lazarus died. No man came to Jesus asking for a resurrection. It was Mary and Martha who came to Him with faith and love and begged him to raise their brother. And Jesus wept and Lazarus came forth. And when you think of Jesus, how did the King come into the world as a baby? Through God who begat Him and the woman Mary who gave birth to Him!"

At those words, the entire throng of women burst forth in cheers and chants, invoking Sojourner Truth's name in rhythmic fashion, their words rising in the air like steam. The young lady who had resisted Mrs. Truth drew near to the stage and touched Frances Gage on the arm.

"My good lady," she said, "I must pass along my deepest regrets that I did not have faith in the person of Sojourner Truth before. God has surely exposed my prejudice and shown me what is good and right!"

"If that is the case," said Mrs. Gage above the din of voices, "then today has been a victory in more ways than one." She smiled and looked around at the adoring crowd. "We've built a movement today, sure as Mrs. Truth shall have a monument to her good work in the future."

Born Isabella Baumfree, **SOJOURNER TRUTH** escaped from slavery with her infant daughter Sophia in 1826, eventually living in New York City as a housekeeper for a Christian minister. A dynamic spiritual experience in 1843 led her to change her name to Sojourner Truth and dedicate her life to traveling and speaking out against the American slavery system. Her memoirs, *The Narrative of Sojourner Truth: A Northern Slave*, were published in 1850. She then joined a speaking tour the next year. Invited to speak at the Ohio Women's Rights Convention in 1851, Truth's speech captivated the audience as she blended the biblical doctrine of the image of God with equal rights for Blacks and women. During the American Civil War, she helped recruit Black soldiers for the Union army. In 2009, one-hundred-twenty-six years after her death, Sojourner Truth was honored with a memorial bust of her likeness in the U.S. Capitol, making her the first African-American woman to have a statue in that historic building.

ROBERT MOFFAT

December 1857, Kuruman, Cape Colony, Africa

The setting sun would have its way, thought the missionary as he walked along the edge of the Tswana settlement near the trees. Robert Moffat was feeling every one of his sixty-two years of age. The rays of the golden orb in the sky poked through the leaves and adorned the area with its warmth as the local inhabitants scoured their food stores for the evening meal. The excitement of the village was pulsing everywhere, and yet Moffat knew that the news he would bring that evening would provide more celebration for the tribe.

Approaching his simple, yet clean and dry, hut, Moffat sidled through the door and saw his wife Mary preparing the meal. He had smelled the scent of pounded goat meat, salt, and oil from many yards away, and his mouth watered at the prospect of the delicious meal. He also knew that in the Tswana tribes, it was customary for the men to prepare the *seswaa*, and so he rebuked himself for not being gifted in cooking as many in the village. Mary smiled at him and pointed to the table.

"Once we thank the Lord, you can begin, Robert," she chirped, mashing a handful of morama beans in one bowl and then placing a crushed, soupy mixture in another. "You'll need your strength for later."

Robert looked in the second bowl, then at his wife. "Mary, you certainly have developed quite the liking for this over the years."

"The mopane worms are delicious," sniffed Mary, "and healthy. I haven't heard you complain of illness since we began eating them regularly after Hagwi made them for us." She dropped a cloth napkin at each of their places and sat across from Robert. "Plates are on the table and the bairns are out playing with their friends. We can enjoy a quiet meal, the two of us, if you'll pray over our food."

Robert reached across the table and took Mary's hands in his own. "Heavenly Father," he prayed, "we give you thanks for this day. We give You thanks for the news we get to share with those to whom You called us. We praise Your name for this food and for the strength it gives us to serve You worthily and love You more deeply. In the name of Christ we pray, Amen."

They began their meal with a couple of minutes in companionable silence. Mary knew from the many years of their marriage that Robert enjoyed thoughtfulness at the beginning of their dinner. He had been excited at the prospect of ministering among the Tswana from the time they had left Britain, and his willingness to endure hardship had not been lost on the tribe amongst whom they now dwelt. His desire to eat the local food had been a slow turn, but Mary was glad to see, after many false starts Robert had finally embraced the local cuisine, marking him as one aligned with the Tswana.

"I am to meet with Hagwi before the assembly," he said wearily, before placing another scoop of meat and beans in his mouth. Swallowing his bite, he continued, "He is tremendously excited, and I hope the entire tribe will be as well."

"You have labored for so long, dear Robert," replied Mary, "that I can hardly believe the day is here. But you truly have nothing to worry about. We and the tribe have become family to each other." She brushed a stray hair from her blue dress. "The women come to me to learn how to sew and make clothes. The children come to you for instruction. The menfolk have always been delighted to experience your gifts of craftsmanship. It was one thing to retain your gardening skills from days gone by in Scotland. It is another altogether to see your carpentry and smithing talents grow and flourish."

"A builder and blacksmith in Africa was something that—if you asked me twenty years ago—I did not think I would be," Robert grunted, the food bringing energy to his weary body. He looked as his dear bride. "You really are God's gift to me. You know that."

Mary shook her curls. "Away with you, my husband. You are becoming very dewy-eyed and soft. It's not like you."

"But you love it all the same," Robert smiled.

"I do," Mary agreed, "but finish your dinner. I am sure Hagwi will come to escort us to the assembly before too long."

Hagwi was punctual as always. His long fingers waved in the air as he gestured excitedly during their walk to the assembly place. "To think of what we have to tell them!" he exclaimed. His loose-fitting and colorful tunic—made by Mary several years ago—was flowing around the stocky contours of his body. "This has been such a long time to receive such a gift." Turning to Robert and Mary as they kept pace with him, Hagwi asked, "Did you ever believe such a day would come?"

"All I can think of is of the first day we came here years ago," Robert grinned as they stepped over a massive tree root sprawled along the path, his hands grasping a large bag. "There was enough hostility to start a brush fire over the entire plain!" After several more steps, he continued, "Then again, your people had not had much reason for trusting us!"

Hagwi nodded, "You and Mary arrived and faced our chief with the sun beating down on the whole tribe and every able-bodied male surrounding you with spears drawn. I had lived only sixteen years at the time and I still remember that moment as if it happened yesterday. Your pale skin and dark beard made us all believe you had come in judgment and desired to destroy us with a single word."

"In fairness to all of you," Mary said, "you had experienced a great deal of abuse from explorers before. We looked the part, so no wonder you did not trust us."

"We had been having such wonderful summer rains for the crops," Hagwi replied wistfully, "and then you arrived and the clouds departed. The rain we thought we needed was gone, and the chief was certain that the clouds dispersed because the white man came." He clapped Robert on the shoulder. "I often wonder and worry what our lives would have become if we had killed you that day."

"The chief demanded we leave the tribe, leave the country," Robert remembered. "And I wondered if this was it, if this was our end, if God had indeed appointed it."

"I will never forget your words," Hagwi shook his head at the memory. "You said to the chief and the soldiers assembled, *'I love you all, we love you! We have a desire from God to serve you, and we cannot leave you as you now are!'* And you spread your hands and left your chest unguarded and said, *'Here, thrust your spear into my heart, and then my wife and our family and companions will know it is time to leave, but we will not leave you unless we are forced to do so!'* Mary, you also showed so much calm in your eyes. All of you did. And then the chief dropped his own spear and said, *'These people ... they do not fear death as we do! There must be something of the immortal in them. Can we refuse them who desire to dwell among us?'* And since then, you have been family."

The tribe had assembled in great numbers in the clearing, as many as were able, and the disappearance of the sun had given relief from the heat. Even after many years, Robert was still amazed at the inverse of seasons, how warming temperatures in the Southern Hemisphere occurred around Christmas. So different from Scotland, he thought. Hagwi quieted the crowd with a gentle wave of his hands and then addressed them all with Robert and Mary at his side as the torches gleamed on the periphery of the crowd and illuminated the darkness.

"My people!" he called out. "We usually gather together as one to worship our Lord Jesus Christ, but tonight we do not gather for church. We have great news, wonderful news to tell you about a work done in our midst.

"I have lived years alongside Robert and Mary, and I am blessed to call them my friends, my family. Their compassion for us has been greater than our hostility when they first arrived. I am sure, Robert, Mary, that coming to dwell here required both strong stomachs and tender hearts. We had been ravaged by enemies, were distrustful of white men and women, and were resistant to the story of Jesus Christ that you shared among us. And yet you did not give up. Over time, one and two, then several, then dozens of us listened to you, and God broke our hearts of stone so we could believe in Jesus! You changed our villages, showed us how to plant food and harvest it well, showed our women how to make clothes, and the men to build tables and chairs. Those may seem to be little things; to us they were great acts of love. Our tradition taught us to stay away from the sick, and to disdain the dead. Yet when illness ravaged our community you entered into our homes, fed us, bathed us, touched us, healed us, and when any died, you buried them properly and prayed for their grieving families. No one had ever showed our people the love that we now know comes through Jesus Christ our Savior. And you have not only given us hope, you have instructed us in the message God has sent. Now, you will share how that has become more."

Stepping back, Hagwi gave space for Robert to come forward. Moving slowly, Robert set the bag on the ground at his feet and looked around at the people. People whose lives were forever changed. People whose eyes had been cold and wary now possessed eyes that were soft and hopeful.

"When we first arrived here, my dear friends," he proclaimed, "all we could see of each other was how different we were. And as time has gone on, over thirty years, we have seen how God has made us more alike than we ever could have dreamed." The tears were flowing now, trickling into his shaggy beard. "However differently God has made us, I look out tonight and see people together who are one people, washed in the blood of the Lamb, Jesus Christ!"

The people cheered loudly for several moments until Robert raised his hand to continue. "Of special remembrance has been not only our preaching of Jesus' Gospel, not only our manual labor and help among you and learning from you, but also learning your speech, your language, so I could seek to bring the Scriptures of our God to you, to understand, to be led by them, and to love God with all your heart.

"That was not without difficulty," Robert went on, "for Tswana has been a spoken language and no one had written it down. And if I recall correctly, learning from you was hard at times, for some—and I say this now with fond memories—would intentionally teach me the wrong words simply to hear me say absurd and profane things." The people tittered at the memory as Robert turned. "Hagwi, I seem to recall you did that on more than one occasion," he laughed.

"I admit my guilt," smiled Hagwi, remembering. "I hope I am still forgiven."

Drawing Hagwi toward him on one side and Mary to his other, Robert replied, "You are more than forgiven, Hagwi. You and your people are beloved. From those labors, we were able to give you a spelling book so you could see Tswana as written. We produced a catechism to teach one another about the salvation in Jesus. From our efforts, we translated the New Testament of Scripture into Tswana. The years went by. There was favor. There was hardship. We gained children. We lost children. We have lived together with you. We have endured the death of some among you. And the work has gone on. That is what I desire to bring to you tonight. I completed it this afternoon on the printing press we brought with us at our arrival. I want to show you what God in His mercy has provided!"

Bending over, Robert reached into his bag and produced from it a pile of papers as the assembly gasped together. Holding it forth, his eyes brightened and he called out in a loud voice, "Previously, we had the Tswana New Testament. By God's grace, we just finished translating the Old Testament. My brothers, my sisters, beloved by Jesus our Lord ... Here is the entire Bible, all of Scripture, that you may read it, believe it, and love the One who spoke it of old!"

The crowd erupted in cheers and song. Those who could began leading chants and songs and dances, and Robert found himself hugged by Hagwi on one side and Mary on the other. And through the din of noise, he heard his wife say, "Amen, my love. What a miracle. What a joy, that Christ has done this through us."

"Indeed, Mary," Robert said, holding her tight. "May He be ever praised."

The Scottish missionary **ROBERT MOFFAT** (1795-1883) left the British Isles in 1816, commissioned by the London Missionary Society to evangelize the area of South Africa. Four years later, he and his wife Mary left Cape Town and went further inland, settling among the native tribes near Kuruman (in modern-day Botswana). The Moffats labored for several years without noticeable impact, but soon, the light of the Gospel shone in that territory. Soon, many responded to Robert's preaching and instruction, people in the Batswana tribe were baptized and received Communion, and Robert set about providing written translations of the Tswana (also known as Setswana) tongue. He produced the first Bible in Tswana and, when he left Kuruman for good in 1870, he left behind a rich legacy of missionary effort and loving care for people who needed to discover the saving grace of Jesus Christ.

HUDSON TAYLOR

1868, Yangzhou, China

The gathering room was a pleasant place to be, thought Hudson Taylor, as the small party milled around drinking their tea and chatting amicably. The August air was considerably muggy both outside and in, but Hudson made a point of wearing the clothes of the locals, and the thin fabric was a welcome relief from the summer heat. He walked over to where his wife Maria was speaking to their fellow mission workers, stirring his tea in the delicate cup.

"There you are," Maria said. "Emily here was just saying it was warmer for four o'clock than normal."

"You choose your garb well for the occasion, Hudson," said Emily Bletchley, who served as the secretary for the China Inland Mission. "For every occasion, as a matter of fact."

"Those are very kind words," Hudson said, giving Maria's hand a squeeze. "Louise, it is good you could stay for tea and then dinner."

"Truth be told," Louise Desgraz replied, "this is a good place to be. I came through the city and there were some crowds gathering and starting to raise their voices. I don't know what the subject was, but their voices were certainly quite strident."

Hudson frowned at the news. "I haven't heard anything of that nature, and I tend to receive regular communication from the prefect or viceroy. I wonder what they were gathering for." He saw the men at the east end of the room waving him toward the door. "Excuse me for a moment."

He walked in their direction, passing William and Mary Rudland on the way and raising his cup to them. Arriving near the window, he took a sip of tea and said, "George? Henry? Even I could see you looked concerned from all the way across the room, and my eyesight is not the best."

"Shh," Henry Reid raised his hand, his head tilting toward the window. "I didn't want to alarm the ladies in the room, but listen. Can you hear that?"

Hudson pressed his ear to the window and sensed it, a rumbling that was growing deeper and coming closer.

"We just heard from one of the servants," George Duncan said, keeping his voice at a whisper. "Some British foreigners came across the river from Zhenjiang and were accosted by the local gentry. All sorts of accusations were hurled at them. We don't know the details, but there are crowds rumbling around and their emotions are at a fever pitch!"

"What are you telling me this for?" asked Hudson, nervously.

"Listen again!" Henry demanded, and when Hudson drew near to the glass it sounded as if the rumble had cut the distance in half. Henry clutched Hudson by the arm. "If we have to leave this room, this place, for safety's sake, what routes do we take?"

Hudson was confused but the rumble in the distance had shifted to a roar and he knew he did not have much time. "There is a short stairwell," he replied, "in the northwest corner. The first door leads onto the roof overlooking the garden. There is a ladder on the roof, and you can place it so anyone can climb down and run through the garden and beyond to escape. The lower door goes to the road winding around, but that would eventually place us in the path of whatever is coming this way." His heart began to race and he uttered a silent prayer. *Lord Jesus, help us and protect us. What is happening?*

As he tendered the prayer, a shout rose from the outer courtyard and a rock smashed through the window above where the Rudlands were standing. The women in the room shrieked with terror and scrambled about. His adrenaline pumping at full force, Hudson spread his hands wide in a calming gesture.

"Maria!" he said in a controlled tone. "You, Emily, and Louise gather the children from their rooms and make for the stairs." He pointed to the corner. He waved the Rudlands in the same direction. "You as well!" Reaching the door of the stairs with his wife, he took Maria's hand. "My love," he said assuringly, "I need to calm the mob and seek help. I pray that I will be successful."

Maria took both his hands in hers and placed them on her swollen belly, the evidence of being six months pregnant. "I will pray you will too, Hudson, for my sake and the sake of our little one." Her voice was choked, halting.

Looking at George and Henry, he sized them up. "George, come with me to the courtyard so we can see what is happening. If there is a large crowd and they are angry, we'll speak to them. They know you and me. They are unfamiliar with Henry, so Henry, you go with the others and provide help for their escape, if need be."

"Are you out of your mind, Hudson?" Henry growled as two more rocks smashed through windows and clattered on the floors, bringing screams from the women. "You don't know if they will kill you or not?"

"Then I will have to find out," Hudson implored him, pushing Henry in the direction of the others, "Take the road over the bridge to Zhenjiang and get to the consulate.[1] George!" He gathered himself and George Duncan nodded and turned with him. "Let us reason with whoever is there."

1. A consulate is a place where diplomats representing another nation are stationed.

The outer courtyard of the mission house was filling with more and more people, many holding stones and clubs and seething with rage. Hudson and George approached the gate and saw the keepers were white with fear.

"Don't be frightened," Hudson reassured them, "but let us through so we can speak with them. And please attempt to send a messenger to the viceroy."[2]

"Master Taylor," one gatekeeper said, "that is not a crowd given to reason."

"Just do as he asks," George Duncan muttered and then, as Hudson slipped through first, turned to the keeper and said, "but be prepared to let us back in at a moment's notice."

Hudson and George approached the assembly of what seemed to be hundreds. Raising his hands, Hudson asked, "What is the trouble? We dwell in peace here among you and we see nothing but rage on your faces. Can you please explain why you have entered our dwelling?"

He never saw the first rock that hurtled through the air and smashed into his temple.

"Mother!" whispered little Samuel to Maria. "Where is Father?"

Pressing his head to her shoulder, Maria fought back the tears. "He went out to speak to the people who have some questions," she replied, her voice stinging at how she had to soften the truth for her own son. "We have to wait until he returns."

"Mrs. Taylor," Henry Reid said softly in the cramped stairwell. "I really don't know how much time we have. We must consider our escape."

How Hudson and George managed to reach the yamen[3] they would never know. Stumbling, bleeding, and bruised,

2. A viceroy would be a Chinese governmental officer in charge of the surrounding province as a representative of the king.

3. A yamen was the residence of a local mandarin (government official) in China.

they sprawled into the outer courtyard past the gatekeepers as part of the mob chased them and kept pelting them with rocks.

"Imagine if more had pursued us!" exclaimed George.

"The fact many are still at the mission house means the lives of my family and our friends are endangered!" Hudson barked as he picked himself off the ground. "Quickly! Inside. I have a plan." Running as hard as he could, Hudson sprinted through the doors of the yamen along with George, barging into the judgment hall and finding himself face to face with the prefect's servants. Their shocked expressions told Hudson that meeting two battered British citizens face to face was an unexpected matter for all of them.

Raising his hands as the mob crashed through the gate outside, Hudson cried out, "Kiu ming! Kiu ming!"[4]

Back at the mission house, Emily and Louise heard the snapping of wooden beams. Flames were rising around the structure of the mission compound. Looking out a small window from the turret, Emily saw the awful truth.

"They are surrounding the house!" she cried. "We have to go out the upper door to the roof, jump, and hope for the best!"

Nearly three hours passed by for Hudson and George. In that time, the prefect[5] met with them, heard their tale of woe silently, and said nothing for several moments. Suddenly, and with great anger in his voice, the prefect asked, "What do you really do with the babies?"

"The babies?" asked the befuddled George.

"Silence!" roared the prefect, pointing to Hudson. "I ask him! What of our babies that you foreigners steal and kill and turn into medicine for yourselves?"

---

4. Translated as "Save life! Save life!", it is a plea that any Chinese official had to obey at any time.

5. A prefect was an official in charge of keeping the peace.

"What are you ..." began George, but Hudson quieted him with a steady outstretched hand.

"My good prefect," Hudson said quietly, "you have been hearing and believing false rumors. No foreigner, whether we who have lived here among you for some time or those who come here to tour these majestic cities, is doing that. Your people have taken the sad reality of the several infants who died at the Catholic orphanage in this city and have grown the story with ideas that are not true! You assume that we British and French and others here have killed your children, when we have not. We are innocent of this charge. But I can tell you that what is happening now at our mission is most certainly true. The gentry of this city have stirred up the people like angry, deadly hornets, and they are attacking our mission and threatening our families there! We have come to you for help, risking our own lives and limbs, broken and bruised. Now will you send your men to help save us?"

"Maria!" Henry Reid called out over the roar of the fires. "The crowd is approaching this end quickly! You'll have to jump from the roof, and I'll catch you!"

"Are you out of your mind?" Maria screamed back, but a brief glance over her shoulder told her she had no other option as the mob pressed closer. She touched her belly and prayed. *Lord, keep me and our little child safe.* She slipped as she flung herself off the roof to the ground below toward Henry's waiting arms.

The fires gave Henry an outline of enough light to see Maria hurtling toward him and he stretched out his hands. Just as she fell into his arms, a brick hurtled into his field of vision. He felt the pain and tasted blood as the brick crushed his eye.

It was wiser, Hudson thought, to go around to the far side of the mission, closer to Zhenjiang. He was hopeful—but not very—that they could meet the rest of his family and the others on the road. Yet they were not hopeful of the speed of the prefect's armed force. The sun was going down and the light in the trees was rather tricky. It was only when they heard a twig snap and saw a movement in the gathering twilight that George pointed thirty yards away. "Look! Over there!"

It was the group! They were frightened and injured. Some, like the Taylor's eldest, Herbert, had twisted ankles from running away on uneven ground. Henry's eye was swollen shut, unrecognizable from the impact of the brick. Maria ran toward Hudson, threw her arms around him, and sobbed.

"It's over, Maria, it's over," he assured her. "I'm here. Let's keep going."

She brushed her tears away and looked back toward the burning mission as the rest of the party trudged down the road toward Zhenjiang. "What is going to happen now? What are we to do?"

Taking her by the arm, Hudson ducked a low-hanging tree branch and followed the rest of their group. "We commit ourselves again, sweet one," he replied with a tired smile. "China will not be won for Christ if we love our ease and comfort above His call."

Four months later, Hudson walked through another courtyard inspecting the newly-gained supplies. The boards and bricks were piled perfectly in the corner, and in spite of the frigid air, Hudson was already thinking through what they could start building in the few days remaining before Christmas. They had their home back, along with a new location for the mission. He rubbed his unshaven face and scratched the stubble. He sensed the pain run through his body as he felt as if he'd aged twenty years in the last months. Yet, in the midst of all the hardship, Hudson had refused any money or restitution from the Chinese. He had spoken no word of blame. "I wish you to know we bear you no ill will," he had told the government officials a month before, "and we desire to give you Christ, not take from your pockets."

"Lost in your thoughts?" came the sweet voice of his wife Maria, who had sidled up to him unnoticed.

"Amazed by the Lord's provision," Hudson said. He placed his arm around Maria, who held baby Charles, born three weeks before. "Zeng Guofan came here earlier. He apologized for the slow response to the riot, as a fine viceroy would have done. He is still amazed we are not insisting on any money to rebuild. I told him it is as it should be."

"You likely did not miss the chance to pave a path to the Cross, my dear husband," Maria smiled, leaning into her husband.

Hudson nodded, stroking little Charles' forehead as his son babbled softly. "Indeed, I told him our Jesus sacrificed so much more to redeem us. We will always desire to become nothing for His sake."

HUDSON TAYLOR (1832-1905) was the foremost Protestant missionary to the Far East in the nineteenth century. Founder of the China Inland Mission in Yangzhou, Taylor, his family, and fellow workers labored to bring the Gospel to regions of that country that were untouched by other missionary efforts. Working with a variety of Christians from different denominations, Taylor was also known for his love of the Chinese and sensitivity to their culture. He wore native Chinese clothing as a point of contact with local people. His zeal for others to trust Jesus Christ was added to a passion to proclaim the Gospel clearly, and so he became able to preach in several dialects of the Chinese language. Despite hardships like the Yangzhou riot, as well as the deaths of his first wife and a number of his children, Taylor remained faithful to Christ through much adversity until his own passing in 1905.

FACT FILES

The Gospel in Difficult Places

You don't have to read too far into the Bible before you realize God's people can go through very difficult experiences. The Hebrews spent over four hundred years as slaves in Egypt before escaping under Moses. David was constantly on the run as he was harassed and hunted by the jealous King Saul. And even Jesus, the night before his death, told his disciples they would be targeted and hated by others merely for being faithful followers of Jesus and proclaimers of his Gospel.

The hardships for Christians can also extend beyond biblical times. During the years that are covered in this book, several individuals stepped out in faith and sought to bring the message of Christ into what might be called "difficult landscapes". Some of these attempts were close to home; others involved travels half a world away. But they all faced particular hardships as they tried to be faithful to Christ.

The ministry of **Hans Egede** (1686-1758) took him to the world's largest island, which happened to be a vast sheet of ice! Born in Harstad, Norway, a community 150 miles north of the Arctic Circle, Egede served as a Lutheran pastor in nearby Vagan. While there, Egede read of old Christian settlements on the gigantic island of Greenland, but there had been no contact with Europe since the early fifteenth century. Egede was struck with a passion to travel to Greenland and establish contact with these settlements and, if none remained, evangelize the Greenlanders himself. Seeking permission from King Frederick IV of Denmark-Norway[1], Egede received

1. Denmark and Norway were a union under a common monarchy from 1537 until 1814.

support for his mission when he included trading ventures and exploration of Greenland's resources. Arriving with his wife and sons in 1721, Egede found Greenland to be an unforgiving, polar landscape where European settlements had long died out and the island inhabited solely by Inuit peoples.[2] Even though what he found was not what he imagined, Egede patiently went about learning the language and culture of the Greenlanders as much as he could so he could share the Gospel with them. In spite of little early success, Egede showed his compassion to the Greenlandic people in 1733 when smallpox killed many Inuit there. Egede and his family cared for the sick and buried the dead, mourning with the families. His actions had a significant effect on the Inuit, who eagerly listened to the Christian message as many put their faith in Christ. Egede also produced a translation of the Bible in Greenlandic and showed great sensitivity for the Inuit culture in doing so. For instance, in the Lord's Prayer in Matthew 6, Egede refrained from using the words "Give us this day our daily bread", for bread was unknown among the Greenlanders. But seal meat was plentiful as a staple item, so Egede rephrased it as "Give us this day our daily seal" to emphasize dependence on God for provision of basic needs. In time, a thriving Christian community arose in Greenland, where Egede founded the town Godthab[3], meaning "Good Hope". For his efforts, Egede became known as the "Apostle of Greenland."

Although we have encountered **Francis Asbury** (1745-1816) in another chapter, he deserves mention here for his diligent labor on the American frontier. Born in Staffordshire, England, Asbury was selected by John Wesley to be a traveling preacher throughout the English countryside for the emerging Methodist Church. His

2. The Inuit are indigenous Arctic people also known to some as Eskimos.
3. Today, Godthab is known as Nuuk, which serves as the capital of Greenland.

faithfulness in that assignment led to a chance to travel to America in 1771, where Asbury spent the next forty-five years of his life establishing Methodist churches in what was the thinly populated area of America west of the Appalachian Mountains. He kept a carefully compiled journal of his travels, providing much data about the towns and communities as America expanded westward. Consecrated as a Methodist bishop by Wesley, Asbury traveled more than a quarter million miles on horseback or by carriage, and he crossed the Appalachians nearly sixty times during his ministry in the United States. He strategically used his travels and organizational abilities to form networks of new churches, called districts. Each of these districts would be served by "circuit riders", Methodist preachers who journeyed through rural areas to preach at various churches. Asbury was especially concerned for spiritual life on the American frontier. The difficulty he saw facing people was the remote nature of their dwellings. In the late eighteenth century, almost all Americans lived in locations of populations under 2,500 people. Many did not have easy access to a church or ministers. Asbury's concern that people should be taught, spiritually guided, and shepherded extended to the frontier, and the multiplication of churches in areas like Tennessee and Kentucky was the result of Asbury's tireless efforts.

Although **Søren Kierkegaard** (1813-1855) was neither a pastor nor a missionary, he found a different path to work out his faith. Born in Copenhagen, Denmark, Kierkegaard was known for marching to the beat of his own drum. Studying theology and philosophy, Kierkegaard wanted to live a life of meaning. He famously said, "What I really need to do is to get clear about what I must do, not what I must know...What matters is to find a purpose, to see what it really is that God wills me to do.

The crucial thing is to find a truth which is truth for me, to find the idea for which I am willing to live and die." He believed that to be an authentic human being, one must seek the truth and live it out with all one's heart, passionately and consistently.

Kierkegaard was a complicated person. Although he wanted to live life with passion, he also made radical decisions to keep himself focused on this vision. He broke off an engagement with his fiancé, Regine Olsen, and later wrote of that experience, comparing it to Abraham's command to sacrifice his son Isaac. He was especially critical of the Lutheran Church in Denmark, which was controlled by the government. He was also grieved that many in the state church were focused on intellectual scholarship and critique of the Bible. Kierkegaard believed if God was truly beyond our comprehension, we couldn't reduce God to small, digestible proofs. Distressed that the state church hummed along on a rhythm of routine, Kierkegaard protested that one could never find true salvation within such a dead institution. Christianity, he wrote, was not a reducible teaching to be swallowed unthinkingly, but rather a life to be experienced by exhilarating risk in a personal relationship with Jesus Christ. Any church that did not have this hope at its heartbeat, Kierkegaard believed, was not truly Christian.

Kierkegaard could be sarcastic and biting in his communication, and this could alienate some readers and listeners rather than help him connect with them. In his radical insistence on "subjective truth" (relating authentically to the truth), he sometimes seemed to downplay "objective truth" (the Scriptural doctrines that God calls us to receive into our minds). Although he did not intend for this to set one's personal ideas over the Bible, this approach can lead in that direction. However,

Kierkegaard bravely stood up against a Danish state church that had gone cold in its doctrine and passion. He showed that sometimes one's calling is to awaken God's people to faithfulness in the place one already lives.

While Kierkegaard stayed close to home, **David Griffiths** (1792-1863) went from one end of the world to the other! A native of south Wales, Griffiths came to faith in Jesus Christ at an early age and began to preach regularly before he turned eighteen. After ten years of ministry and only a few months of marriage to his bride Mary, Griffiths was assigned to missionary work in Madagascar by the London Missionary Society. Arriving there in early 1821, Griffiths founded the first Protestant church in that island nation. He and Mary made a dedicated team. She taught girls in schools, and he instructed boys while also preaching twice every Sunday. With the permission and blessing of King Radama I, Griffiths set about providing Christian materials in the Malagasy language.

Griffiths managed to secure the use of a printing press, creating a letter alphabet system of the Malagasy language and publishing a catechism[4] and a hymnal. After Radama's death, Griffiths completed the translation of the New Testament and much of the Old in the Malagasy tongue. This was significant as it was the first time the Bible had been published in an African language. Not long after these events, a fierce persecution arose against Christians, and Griffiths—at first sentenced to death—was exiled from Madagascar. He and his family returned to Britain, where he pastored churches but never forgot the people of Madagascar. He continued his translation work, revising the Malagasy Bible and also translating other works—including John

4. A catechism is a book or document of questions and answers designed to instruct people (primarily children) in the essentials of the Christian faith.

Bunyan's *Pilgrim's Progress*—into that language. He also wrote books about the general history of Madagascar and of the persecution of Christians on that island. These works opened the hearts and minds of British people to events at the other end of the world.

Finally, one person who went headlong into hard times was **John Duncan** (1796-1870). Born in Aberdeen, Scotland, Duncan was an interesting case of someone who studied theology although he was an atheist at the time. Even after being ordained to the ministry, Duncan believed that God existed, yet he had not yet had a conversion experience of repentance and faith. Later, he placed his trust in Christ while influenced by the preaching of Cesar Malan, a Swiss pastor who was visiting Britain at the time.

His comprehensive understanding of Hebrew, Syriac, and many other Middle Eastern languages earned Duncan the nickname of "Rabbi"[5] and also opened the door for a most unusual venture in 1840. The Church of Scotland had developed an interest in Christian mission to Jewish people. Knowing of Duncan's own interest in Israel and love of all things Hebrew, the Church named him a missionary to the Jews and deployed him to Budapest, Hungary, to minister among the Jewish population in that capital city. Rabbi Duncan undertook his work with joy and vigor, and his gracious manner and knowledge of the Old Testament Hebrew Scriptures made him a beloved figure there. His work was not without struggle, but a number of Jews were converted to Christianity as the result of his preaching and warm friendship. Alfred Edersheim—who would write *The Life and Times of Jesus the Messiah*—was one of Duncan's converts. In addition, Duncan's patient teaching and kindness worked in the hearts of Israel Saphir, a Jew

5. *Rabbi* is the Hebrew word for "teacher".

respected for his wisdom in the Budapest community, and his son Adolph. They embraced the Gospel of Jesus, and Adolph himself became a Presbyterian missionary. There was a good bit of resistance from the Jewish people in Budapest to Duncan's work, but he kept at it and enjoyed fruitful results of many people coming to Christian faith in the three years he spent there. Even after Duncan returned to Scotland, where he spent years as a professor of Hebrew at New College in Edinburgh, Scotland, he retained his love for the Jewish people, exhibiting his faith always with tenderness, wisdom, and humility.

DWIGHT MOODY

January 1, 1874, Chicago, Illinois

The four men forced themselves southward along LaSalle Street in the freezing cold. Bundled up in their overcoats, the quartet of souls walked briskly past various buildings before coming to an open space at an intersection. There a chilly blast from off Lake Michigan hurled itself at the men nearly knocking one of them into the path of an approaching carriage.

"Your energy is greater than your wits at the moment, Brother Dwight!" barked one of the men above the howling gale. His companion caught his hat as it was being blown off his head.

"Energy is what the Lord gives us to do His work!" exclaimed Dwight Moody, signaling the men to follow him on down LaSalle Street. "We are clustered together, which does wonders for sharing warmth, but it means we are covering much less territory, and time is of the essence. Listen! It would make more sense for us to go our separate ways and do the Lord's work, for we can move over four times as much ground apart as we could together." Pointing at each of them in turn and then off in a different direction, Moody continued. "You, west. You, east. You, back north. I'll go south. Remember, anyone you meet, anyone you encounter: Tell them what a great work is being done at our church and invite people to come. And tell them to bring a friend!"

"We had our first service yesterday," complained one of his companions, "and already you want to scour the city for more people? In the cold?"

Moody clapped him roundly on the shoulder. "Indeed! As our Lord Jesus said in His parable, where the banqueting lord says to his servant, 'Go out in the highways and hedges, and compel them to come in, that my house may be filled'! Our church is the house of the Lord, and if He desires it to be filled with those hungry for the banquet of His Word, then we must seek those who must be brought in! Go, and let us meet back here in an hour to assess our progress!"

The three other men wearily but dutifully set out, amazed by the exuberance of their pastor. As for himself, Dwight Moody sprang into a trot down LaSalle Street. He watched as the horse-drawn carriages moved along in the opposite direction. He had heard of new rail cars helping people traverse the hilly roads of San Francisco and offered a quick prayer to God that such operations could be developed in Chicago. What a joy that would be, he thought, to transport those who could not go to church to come to church!

In quick succession, Moody opened the door of a lunch diner, a grocer market, and a public house. He was not surprised to see these establishments open, even on New Year's Day. In each venue, he went up to the owners and excitedly told them of the Chicago Avenue Church. They had just held their initial services the day before. Could there not be a better way to begin the new year and a new phase of life than for his hearers to come to services at Chicago Avenue Church and hear what Jesus could do to make their lives new and meaningful? To hear how a life of sin could be cleansed by the work of Christ? His listeners tended to be both polite and generally evasive.

"That certainly sounds interesting. I'll see if I have time."

"A new church? Oh, heavens. That seems like a massive undertaking."

"I'm not really seeking for help, but I'm glad you're happy to be helping others. I'll sit this one out, though."

"Been to church before. Didn't help me. But hope you find people you need, preacher."

Moody was saddened by the low-grade resistance but didn't fade in his enthusiasm. His voice peppered each establishment with joy and kindness, even in the midst of being refused.

"Just so you know," he said to many a soul, "the doors of God's house are always open, because His heart is always open to us. May He bless you today." And then he would go right out in the bitter cold to seek more people to invite.

Some people had started to show an interest, although Moody couldn't be sure if they did so from an understanding of their spiritual need or if they were merely curious. Moody chuckled about how he loved the city of Chicago even as friends such as Ira Sankey, who led music in his services, cautioned him that the urban crowds would take much labor to convert. *If God has called me,* Moody thought, *He will provide the harvest He desires.* Moody was so engrossed in his thoughts as he approached another lunch house further south on LaSalle Street that he almost missed the opportunity. And even then, it took a gale force wind to knock him sideways where he happened to look down a dirty alley. And there, he saw him.

He was a quivering mound of humanity, situated under several blankets that—while giving adequate cover—were quite threadbare and offered little in the way of warmth. As Moody crept into the alley, around a trash bin and over several piles of frost-laden refuse, he saw more clearly that the man—seated between two piles of wooden crates—had a salt-and-pepper beard, brambly and wild. A tattered coat covered his torso, from which came a rattling, wheezing sound. Squatting next to him, Moody could see saliva frozen on the man's lips and beard, as one could expect from so many of the city's tramps at this time of year. What struck Moody, though, was not the homeless man's congested cough, his trembling body, or his ramshackle ensemble of clothing and shelter. Looking closely, Moody peered into the man's eyes. They were gray and large, and Moody could hardly believe they also seemed hopeful.

Daring to put the man at ease, Moody reached toward the edge of the blanket and took his hand that gripped the edge of the cover near his collarbone.

"My friend," he said in a placid voice, clear as a bell over the howling wind above them, "my name is Dwight. Might I have the pleasure of knowing you?"

The homeless man's hand shook in Moody's grasp, his fingernails blue and standing out against the chalkiness of his skin. His voice was a barely-audible croak. "Charley," he gasped. "Name's Charley."

The interior of the lunch house was considerably warmer than the frigid streets. Charley coughed violently as he sat down in his chair, the impact dislodging a mix of frost and dirt into the air around him. Moody, unfazed, asked what was on the menu for that day when a thought struck him.

"Ma'am?" he asked the waitress, "is there the possibility you haven't put away your breakfast foods?"

The waitress looked at Moody, then Charley, her face clearly betraying her disturbance by the homeless man's appearance. Turning back to Moody, she gripped the rag in her hands and answered, "We have some. Of course, we'd prefer not to keep it for tomorrow and serve it as fresh as we can. I could offer you a reduced price on the meal. It would be a plate of scrambled eggs, plus sausages, and fried potatoes. I can get you each some coffee, too. Will that be alright?"

Moody's eyes danced as he looked across the table at Charley. "What do you say, Charley? Would you like a solid breakfast?"

"I'd love a solid anything at this time," Charley sputtered, his chest wheezing horribly as he spoke. "Sausages would be a true bonus."

Moody slapped his hands on the table and turned to the waitress. "We'll have two plates of what you just offered, plus two cups of coffee." He lowered his voice. "And the bill comes to me."

The waitress shook her head and whispered, "I don't know why you bother, sir, but you asked for it, so you'll get it."

After she left, Moody turned in Charley's direction as his table mate let loose another cough, spittle flying onto his beard. "Charley, I'm glad that I get to share this meal with you," Dwight said "and I think there's a way I can enjoy it more."

"What's that?" Charley asked with a pained expression.

Moody leaned across the table. "I'd like to know your story, Charley."

"My story?"

"Yes. As surprised as you were to see me today, and as surprised as I guess you are to be sitting in a lunch house sharing a meal, I'd like to surprise you even more. Tell me about your life, where you have lived, what has brought you to this moment."

"My life?" Charley growled, a pain running through his chest as his body continued its slow defrosting. "My life can't be that interesting to anybody."

"Well, I'm asking the question," said Moody, "and I am interested." He stopped as the waitress returned and placed two breakfasts and two cups of black coffee at their places. As she left, he continued, "But before you share your story, allow me to thank the Lord for this food."

"Seems it came from here and not God," grunted Charley, "but go ahead all the same."

"Our Lord Jesus," Moody began, praying comfortably and openly as the other patrons either gaped or ignored them, "I give you thanks for this meal that we are about to share. Cause this food to strengthen our bodies so we might live and serve you well. In your name we pray, Amen."

Charley began wolfing down his potatoes and then attacking his eggs. Moody watched him with some amusement as Charley grasped his spoon and was scooping his food on it time and again. It struck Moody that it had been some time since Charley sat down at a table for a meal. He gave Charley time to eat while he himself picked at his sausages. Finally, he returned to his original question as Charley finished his food and began gulping his coffee, gripping the mug with both hands.

"So, your life, Charley?" he began. "Have you always lived in Chicago?"

Charley looked at Moody, surprised. "Actually, I was born in Milwaukee. A little way, but not terribly far. My parents lived there."

"What did they do?" Moody inquired as he signaled the waitress to bring another plate to Charley. Around them, the other people scowled but said nothing.

Charley raised an eyebrow. "Momma worked in a shop. Pop cleaned windows on the main streets."

Moody took Charley's clipped answers in stride but knew instinctively there was more. "Any brothers? Any sisters?"

"Two brothers, one older, one younger," Charley said gruffly as the exasperated waitress brought a small helping of sausages and potatoes, clattering the plate noisily on the table. Charley suddenly displayed a faraway look in his eyes. "They're both dead. One drowned in Lake Michigan when I was five. The other died of typhoid fever three years later." Moody wasn't sure but he thought Charley's eyes began to moisten.

"And how did you end up here in Chicago?" he asked.

Charley clenched his jaw, not wanting to say but also bidden by Moody's kindness to share his life in a way he never dreamed. "Pop died suddenly one Christmas when I was nineteen. He coughed blood until he wasted away." He paused before continuing. "I was with him as he died. I couldn't bring myself to stay and help my mother. I walked outside, hopped a carriage headed here, went to a saloon, crawled inside a bottle of whiskey, and that's been my home ever since." He stopped. "I don't know why I told you this." His lip quivered. "You take me out of the cold and I just tell you all my past. I'm just humiliated by all of this. I am eating a meal and I've ruined your day."

"Charley," Moody said, "you've blessed my day." Standing, he pulled Charley up from the chair and said, "Come, I've got a place where I wish to take you. Just let me stop here at the door."

"For what?"

"Because I'll pay for our meals."

Charley looked as if he'd been struck by lightning. "You'll what?"

"Give me a moment," Moody said quietly, walking toward the waitress. Paying more than enough for the meals, he turned around to find Charley had disappeared. He was nowhere in the lunch house, as if he'd vanished into thin air!

"Sir?" Moody asked the man at the table nearest him. "Did you happen to see the man I was with? I can't find him!"

"Went out into the street, he did," snorted the man, pointing to the front door, but Moody was already sprinting to get outside by the time the man finished his sentence.

He found Charley curled up at the bottom of the restaurant steps, hunched over his hands as he sat on the frozen sidewalk and rocking back and forth with violent shakes. And Moody could see he was bawling. Drawing near, he sat beside Charley and wrapped his arms around him in a firm embrace.

"Charley, my friend," he said, "tell me why you're crying."

It took some time for Charley to calm down, and when he did, his eyes were bloodshot red and the tears had frozen on his cheeks. "You actually wanted me to eat with you. And then you...you...you paid for my meal!" He began bawling again. "No one has ever bought me a meal in my entire life!"

Moody embraced Charley again, clapping him gently on the back, which brought forth another round of coughing. "Charley, my dear friend, I can introduce you to someone who has done that, yet in a much greater way. Someone who has gone out to people who were lost and hopeless, brought them in for dinner, and paid the debt they owed. And if you'll come with me, I'll make sure you know how much he cares for you."

"You'll introduce me to him?"

"Indeed I will, Charley. His name is Jesus. And he wants to give you the warmest welcome you can imagine."

Charley allowed Moody to pull him to his feet and took his arm as they journeyed northward along LaSalle Street. "I like the idea of warm. I strangely like the idea of meeting Jesus even more," he said as the two men made their way through the brutal cold on the way to Chicago Avenue Church.

The evangelist **DWIGHT MOODY** (1837-1899) was an enthusiastic preacher who delighted in speaking to others about the saving grace of Jesus Christ. Although he traveled to many countries, his effect was felt greatly in America. A successful shoe and boot salesman, he felt compelled to work for the spiritual revival of all whom he met. He worked among Union soldiers in the American Civil War and with the Young Men's Christian Association. Settling in Chicago, he led many people to become followers of Jesus through his commitment to the Bible and his dynamic way with words. Moody founded a church (eventually called the Chicago Avenue Church and now Moody Church) and a Bible college (now Moody Bible Institute) in Chicago that continue to this day. His most enduring quote is "Faith makes all things possible; love makes all things easy."

WHERE WE GET OUR INFORMATION

Aitken, Jonathan. *John Newton: From Disgrace to Amazing Grace.* Wheaton, IL: Crossway Books, 2013.

Brown, Stewart and Timothy Tackett, ed. *The Cambridge History of Christianity: Enlightenment, Reawakening, and Revolution, 1660-1815.* Cambridge, UK: Cambridge University Press, 2008.

Bunyan, John. *Grace Abounding to the Chief of Sinners.* London, UK: The Religious Tract Society, 1905.

Calhoun, David. *In Their Own Words: The Testimonies of Martin Luther, John Calvin, John Knox, and John Bunyan.* Carlisle, PA: Banner of Truth Trust, 2018.

Davis, Walter W. *Eastern and Western History, Thought, and Culture: 1600-1815.* Lanham, MD: University Press of America, 1993.

Dorsett, Lyle W. *A Passion for Souls: The Life of D.L. Moody.* Chicago, IL: Moody Publishers, 2003.

Ferguson, Sinclair. I*n the Year of our Lord: Reflections on Twenty Centuries of Church History*. Orlando, FL: Reformation Trust, 2018.

Gilley, Sheridan and Brian Stanley, eds. *The Cambridge History of Christianity: World Christianities, c. 1815-c. 1914.* Cambridge, UK: Cambridge University Press, 2008.

Gonzalez, Justo. T*he Story of Christianity, vol. 2: From the Reformation to the Present Day.* New York, NY: Harper & Row, 1985.

Jensen, Florence Huntington. *Hearts Aflame.* Waukesha, WI: Metropolitan Church Association, 1932.

Johnson, George D. *What Will a Man Give in Exchange for His Soul?* Bloomington, IN: Xlibris, 2011.

Latourette, Kenneth Scott. *A History of Christianity, Volume II: Reformation to the Present*, rev. ed. Peabody, MA: Prince Press, 1997.

Lawson, Steven J. *Pillars of Grace, A.D. 100-1564: A Long Line of Godly Men.* Ligonier Ministries: Orlando, FL: Ligonier Ministries, 2016.

McGrath, Alister, ed. *The Christian Theology Reader, Third Edition.* Hoboken, NJ: Wiley-Blackwell, 2006.

McGreal, Ian P., ed. *Great Thinkers of the Western World.* New York, NY: Harper Collins Publishers, 1992.

Meadows, Denis. *Five Remarkable Englishmen: A New Look at the Lives and Times of Walter Raleigh, Captain John Smith, John Winthrop, William Penn, and James Oglethorpe.* New York, NY: Devin-Adair, 1961.

Needham, Nick. *2000 Years of Christ's Power, Volume 4: The Age of Religious Conflict.* Ross-shire, UK: Christian Focus Publications, 2016.

Olson, Roger. *The Story of Christian Theology.* Downers Grove, IL InterVarsity Press, 1999.

Packer, J.I. *A Quest for Godliness: The Puritan Vision of the Christian Life.* Wheaton, IL: Crossway Books, 1990.

Piper, John. *The Hidden Smile of God: The Fruit of Affliction in the Lives of John Bunyan, William Cowper, and David Brainerd.* Wheaton, IL: Crossway Books, 2001.

Piper, John and Justin Taylor, ed. *A God-Entranced Vision of All Things: The Legacy of Jonathan Edwards.* Wheaton, IL: Crossway Books, 2004.

Purkiss, Diane. *The English Civil War: Papists, Gentlewomen, Soldiers, and Witchfinders in the Birth of Modern Britain.* New York, NY: Basic Books, 2006.

"Robert and Mary Moffat: Missionaries to South Africa" https://www.wholesomewords.org/missions/bmoffat20.html

Rusten, E. Michael and Sharon. *The One Year Book of Christian History: A Daily Glimpse Into God's Powerful Work.* Wheaton, IL: Tyndale House Publishers, 2003.

Ryken, Leland. *Worldly Saints: The Puritans as They Really Were.* Grand Rapids, MI: Zondervan, 1986.

Samuels, Maurice. "Conspiracy Theories, Class Tension, Political Intrigue: Lessons from France's Mishandling of a 19th Century Cholera Outbreak". https://time.com/5837393/paris-cholera-lessons/ May 15, 2020.

Shelley, Bruce. *Church History in Plain Language.* Nashville, TN: Thomas Nelson, 1995.

Sibbes, Richard. *The Bruised Reed,* rev. ed. Edinburgh, UK: The Banner of Truth Trust, 1998.

Walton, Robert C. *Chronological and Background Charts of Church History.* Grand Rapids, MI: Zondervan, 1986.

Other books in the series:

Redemption

The Church in Ancient Times

Luke H. Davis

The story of the ancient Church is one of a people who were finding their way over many years by the light that God shined forth for them. Today, we are looking back over the centuries with many more years of understanding but we stand on the shoulders of those who braved persecution, death, debate, and mystery on behalf of generations to come. From the Apostle Peter at Pentecost in Jerusalem to St. Patrick on the shores of Ireland in the year 432 – the ancient church has much to teach the church of today.

ISBN: 978-1-5271-0801-1

Reign

The Church in the Middle Ages

Luke H. Davis

During the Middle Ages the church labored to build a community of faith. Benedict, Columba, and Francis organized communities in which the Gospel could be preached. Theodulf, Anselm, and Bernard of Clairvaux answered the call to reform that community and theology. And when the church's leaders drifted from the authority of Scripture, a first wave of reformers in Peter Waldo, John Wycliffe, and John Hus arose to call God's people back to the grace of God.

ISBN: 978-1-5271-0801-1

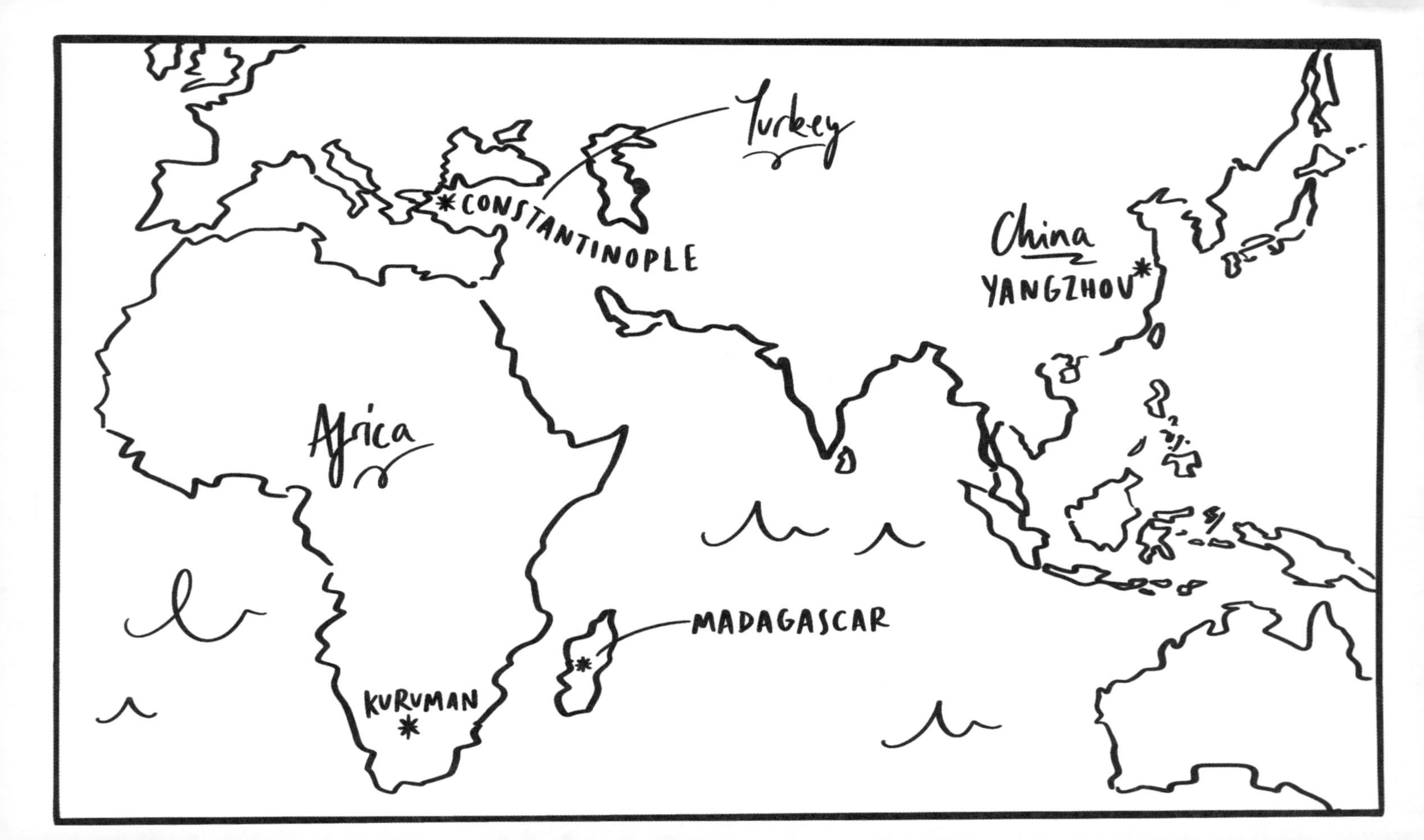
Turkey
CONSTANTINOPLE
China
YANGZHOU
Africa
MADAGASCAR
KURUMAN

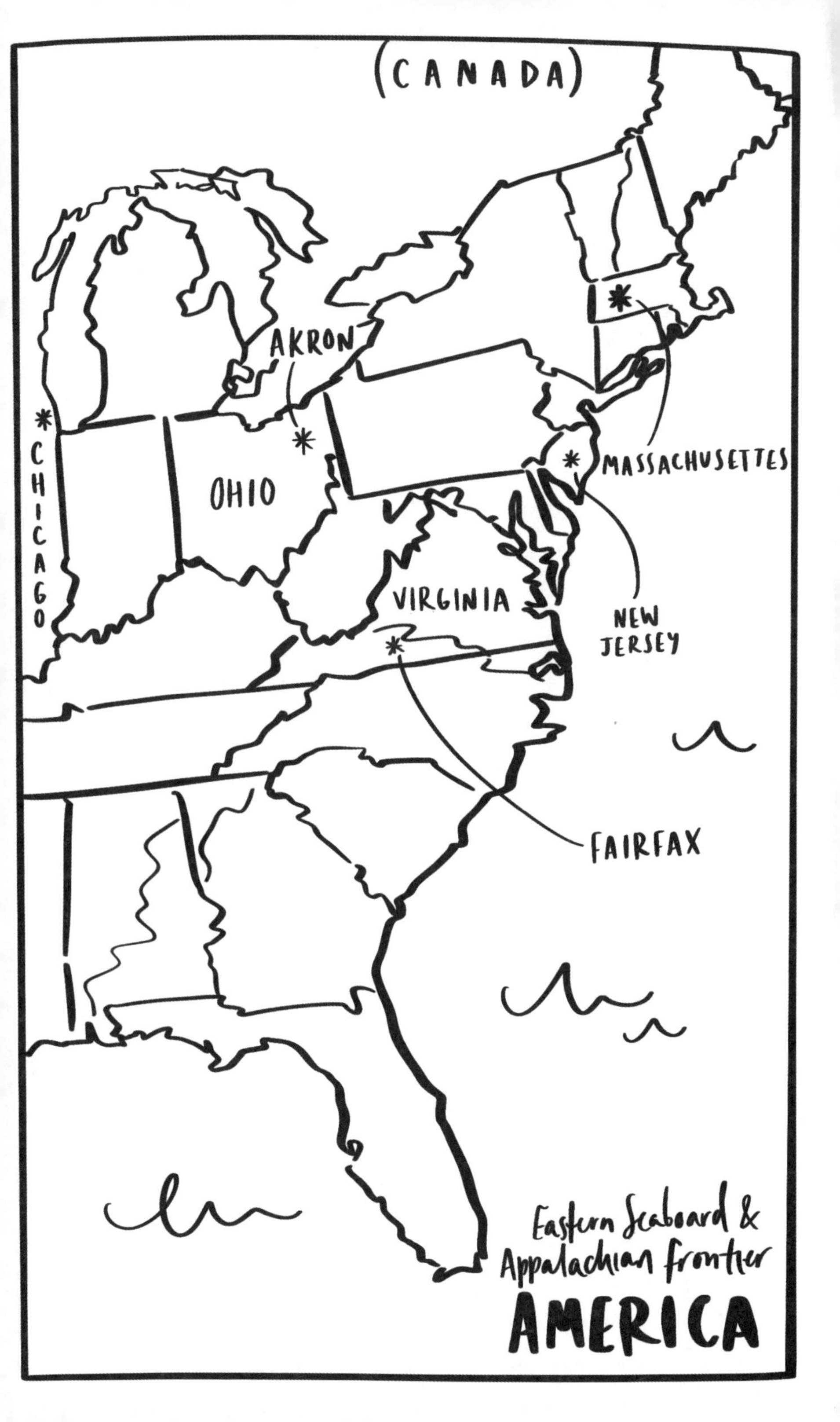
(CANADA)
AKRON
CHICAGO
OHIO
VIRGINIA
MASSACHUSETTES
NEW JERSEY
FAIRFAX
Eastern Seaboard &
Appalachian frontier
AMERICA

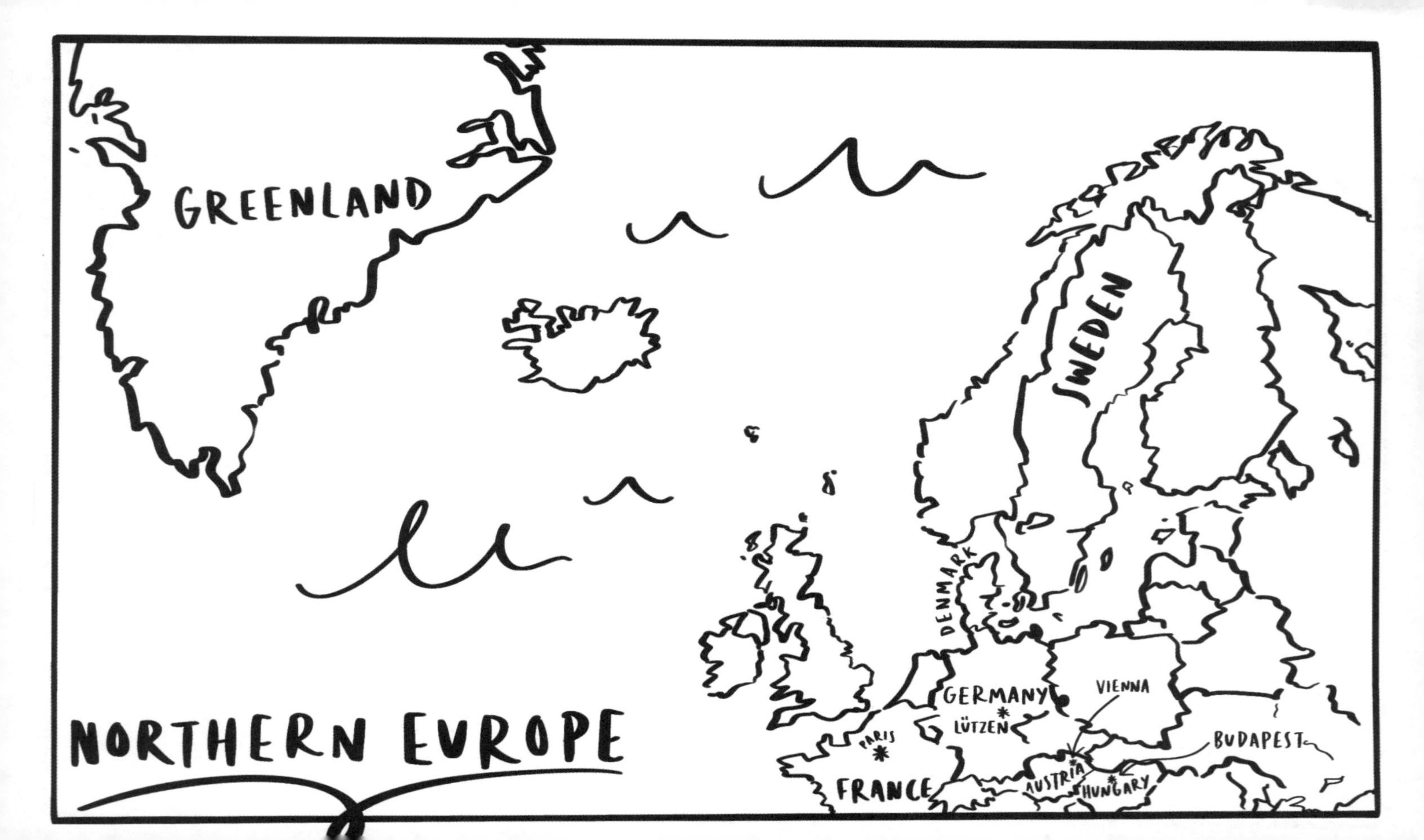
GREENLAND
SWEDEN
DENMARK
GERMANY
LÜTZEN
VIENNA
BUDAPEST
PARIS
FRANCE
AUSTRIA
HUNGARY
NORTHERN EUROPE

EDINBURGH
UK
HULL
BEDFORD
LONDON

Christian Focus Publications publishes books for adults and children under its four main imprints: Christian Focus, CF4K, Mentor and Christian Heritage. Our books reflect our conviction that God's Word is reliable and Jesus is the way to know him, and live for ever with him.

Our children's publication list covers pre-school to early teens. We also publish personal and family devotional titles, biographies and inspirational stories that children will love.

From pre-school board books to teenage apologetics, we have it covered!

Christian Focus Publications Ltd,
Geanies House, Fearn, Ross-shire,
IV20 1TW, Scotland,
United Kingdom.
www.christianfocus.com

Find us at our web page:
www.christianfocus.com

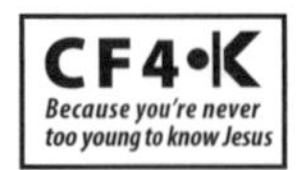